Praise for *Tibetan Shamanism*

"A very interesting and important book by a major authority on contemporary Tibetan shamanism and on shamanism in general. He makes a contribution not just to shamanic studies, but to the preservation of the threatened spiritual heritage of the Tibetans themselves."

— Michael Harner, PhD, author of *The Way of the Shaman* and *Cave and Cosmos: Shamanic Encounters with Another Reality*

"Larry Peters has devoted his life to studying Nepalese shamanism as both an anthropologist and as a practitioner, and so writes with a rare combination of deep personal experience and professional expertise."

— Roger Walsh MD, PhD, University of California, author of *The World of Shamanism*

"Larry Peters has spent decades researching the healing practices in Tibetan shamanism. *Tibetan Shamanism: Ecstasy and Healing* is an ethnography of shamanic healing and the transmutation of soul in a Buddhist culture that ostensibly does not recognize the concept of soul."

— Sandra Ingerman, MA, author of *Soul Retrieval: Mending the Fragmented Self* and *Walking in Light*

"Larry Peters has an intimate knowledge of ecstatic healing methods among Tibetans and Nepalese, and his book shows how close he is to the shamans, and that he has an understanding of their reality made possible by extended field stays. I met many of the people Peters writes about during my stay in Nepal in 1970-'71 and meeting them again in *Tibetan Shamanism* is a most welcome experience."

— Per-Arne Berglie, PhD, professor emeritus, History of Religions, Stockholm University

"I've known Dr. Larry Peters's deep work on the shamanic healing practices of the Tibetan peoples for two decades. Professor Peters's experiential knowledge of this healing tradition makes this book a must read for anyone interested in Tibetan shamanism or shamanism in general."

— Bhola Banstola, Nepalese Shaman, president and founder of Nepal Shaman

TIBETAN SHAMANISM

ECSTASY *and* HEALING

LARRY PETERS, PhD

North Atlantic Books
Berkeley, California

Published by
North Atlantic Books
Berkeley, California

Cover photo by Larry Peters, PhD
Cover design by Daniel Tesser
Book design by Brad Greene

Printed in the United States of America

"Tradition, Practice, and Trance" was originally published as "Tradition, Practice and Trance of the Foundation's Tibetan Living Treasures," in *Shamanism Annual,* Issue 22, December 2009. "Soul in Contemporary Tibetan Shamanism" was originally published in *Shamanism Annual,* Issue 23, December 2012. "Shaman as Psychopomp" was originally published in *Shamanism Annual,* Issue 23, December 2010. "The Tibetan Healing Rituals of Dorje Yüdronma" was originally published in *Shaman's Drum,* Number 45, 1997. "The *Yeti:* Spirit of Himalayan Forest Shamans" was originally published in *Shamanism,* Vol. 18, 2005. "The *Ghe-wa* (Tibetan Death Rite) for Pau Karma Wangchuk Namgyal" was originally published in *Shamanism Annual,* Issue 21, December 2008. All used by permission.

Tibetan Shamanism: Ecstasy and Healing is sponsored and published by the Society for the Study of Native Arts and Sciences (dba North Atlantic Books), an educational nonprofit based in Berkeley, California, that collaborates with partners to develop cross-cultural perspectives, nurture holistic views of art, science, the humanities, and healing, and seed personal and global transformation by publishing work on the relationship of body, spirit, and nature.

North Atlantic Books' publications are available through most bookstores. For further information, visit our website at www.northatlanticbooks.com or call 800-733-3000.

Library of Congress Cataloging-in-Publication Data

Names: Peters, Larry, author.
Title: Tibetan Shamanism : ecstasy and healing / Larry Peters.
Description: Berkeley, California : North Atlantic Books, 2016.
Identifiers: LCCN 2015038279 | ISBN 9781623170301 (pbk.) |
ISBN 9781623170318 (ebook)
Subjects: LCSH: Shamanism—Tibet Region. | Shamanism—Nepal.
Classification: LCC BL2370.S5 P48 2016 | DDC 299.5/4—dc23
LC record available at http://lccn.loc.gov/2015038279

1 2 3 4 5 6 7 8 9 SHERIDAN 20 19 18 17 16

Printed on recycled paper

TABLE OF CONTENTS

Great Stupa. Photo by Larry Peters.

INTRODUCTION

Soul (*la*)[1] fulfills an important role in Tibetan shamanism. Tibetan beliefs regarding the individual's soul (or souls) have changed over the millennia. Before Buddhism, in indigenous shamanism (Bön), there was a belief in an immortal soul. When Buddhism came to Tibet in the mid-eighth century CE, it arrived with very different ideas regarding the soul. Buddhism rejects the existence of a soul. Still, in the "folk religion" of lay culture and in shamanism, the belief in soul persists, albeit how it is viewed has changed due to Buddhism and, a millennium later, due to exile and subsequent acculturation in Nepal.

This book is the result of ethnographic fieldwork that began in 1996 and continued until 2012 when the last of the four Tibetan shamans who are the subjects of this study passed away. I visited the shamans regularly during this sixteen-year period. We became friends and I was privileged to know their families, to observe their healing practices, daily life, and community events, and to be taught their belief system.

As part of my touring business, I would routinely bring students and colleagues to Nepal to study shamanism, and spend two weeks to a month doing field research prior to their arrival and after they left Nepal. These trips averaged three per year. Thus this book is more than a philosophical study of soul. It is a study of soul in the context of shamanic healing, trance states, and the interactive relationship with spirits. In other words, a map of the shamanic spiritual world is described, as are the states of consciousness and the "techniques of ecstasy" necessary to access it.

Research was conducted at two field sites. One is in the town of Boudhanath (Nepali for Lord of Wisdom), about 6 km from Kathmandu, the capital of Nepal, and the location of the Tibetan

Buddhist "Great Stupa" (see Figure 0-1), an ancient place of pilgrimage, a large reliquary structure for the Buddhist saint Mahakasyapa, and a Nepal heritage site. Boudhanath has a population of about 100,000 and is the home of a dozen or so Buddhist monasteries. The second is the Tibetan refugee camp known as Tashi Palkhiel with a population of about 1,200, located outside Pokhara, Nepal's second-largest city, and about 200 km from Kathmandu. At the first site I studied the healing system of Lhamo Dolkar (in this context, *lhamo* means shaman goddess), and at the second, the three male shamans (*lhapa* or *pau*) who lived with their families at Tashi Palkhiel and worked as shamans.

Lhamo Dolkar and Wangchuk, the elder of the three Pokhara shamans, as discussed in this book, were both certified as authentic shaman healers by His Holiness the Dalai Lama. This is of interest in its own right as, prior to exile and the Chinese invasion of Tibet in the 1950s, shamanism was viewed as an apostate religion and its practice suppressed. The enmity toward and violent treatment of shamans by Buddhist lama has a long history in Tibet and neighboring Mongolia. At one point, shamans were burned at the stake (Kingsley 2010).

Prior to exile, shamanism was tenacious in the Himalayan mountainous terrain, especially in difficult-to-reach areas geographically distant from the Buddhist monastic urban centers (Samuel 1993). Despite the current domination of Communist China, shamanism still exists, albeit limited to isolated communities in far northern Tibet (Bellezza 2005). What I discovered was that Tibetan shamanism in exile was not a religion. All the shamans identified themselves as lay Buddhists. The deities the shamans invoke in their healings are indigenous Bön deities converted to Buddhism. Further, there is no community or affiliation between the individual shamans. Each has his or her own practice and can be very critical of the work of other shamans. Shamanism in exile is a spiritual profession, but it is not competitive with Buddhism. In the refugee camp, shamanism was socially tolerated by the lama, but seen as superstition and therefore falling short of "ultimate truth." Worse yet, some camp members fear shamanic practice and believe it to be heretical to Buddhism.

At Tashi Palkhiel, shamanism was a central element in cultural life when the camp was new in the 1960s and '70s (Berglie 1976, 1992). But, as Buddhism became more present, a monastery was constructed, and lama and monks were imported, shamanism lost status and quietly folded into the background of camp life. One of the camp shamans, Nyima, the youngest of them, early in his career, was apprenticed to one or the other two elder shamans at the camp at different times. Aspects of his training were evidence of what was once a robust shamanic practice at the camp. He was one of three disciples, but recently there have been no disciples, and consequently no one receiving training. Tibetan shamanism ceased to exist in the exile community in Pokhara when Nyima died in 2013. Even the children of the shamans, who spent much of their youth witnessing shamanic rituals, follow Buddhism and express little interest in shamanism, something none of them has been "called" to. It seems to me that the cultural diminution of shamanism at Tashi Palkhiel is in many ways analogous to the history of shamanism in Tibet after Buddhism.

The ending is similar in Boudhanath with Lhamo. Here, too, Tibetan shamanism passed when Lhamo died, as she had no disciples. Like the three male shamans in Pokhara at the time of research, Lhamo, too, was dependent upon Western tourism to sustain her practice as a shaman. In other words, Tibetan shamanic practice in exile involved mostly Western clients, some Nepalese, but few Tibetans. Lhamo had a large practice and, most days of the week, she would treat as many as twenty-five clients. Boudhanath and its *stupa* are tourist destinations, and Lhamo had achieved some notoriety. At the camp, the three male shamans had very small practices and often would treat just one or two clients in an entire week, if any at all, unless I (or another group leader) brought students to them for shamanic healing.

Generally speaking, shamanism among the Nepalese is accepted culturally and has a strong foundational belief system. Thus there are numerous Nepalese shamans and a few who are popular. For example, in Boudhanath, there were, during the period in which I studied with Lhamo, at least two other shamans with reasonably large practices. Both of these shamans were Tamang, one of the many Tibetan ethnic groups that have resided in Nepal for centuries, and are citizens, not refugees. Tibetan groups like the Tamang are called Bhotiya (Tibetan) and are distinguished culturally and shamanically from the recent immigrants who fled Tibet in the last sixty years. The latter group is the focus of this book. However, it is worth noting that there are rituals, symbols, and myths that seem to come from a common source. For example, before exile, Wangchuk pilgrimaged many times to one of the sacred Bön mountains, Targo, a place only accomplished Tibetan shamans go to for initiation. It requires entering a cave, ritually invoking the deity of the mountain, and finally climbing a nine-step ladder in order to exit the cave (Bellezza 2005). The final initiation for Tamang shamans in Nepal is called *gufa* (Nepali for cave) and it likewise involves ascending a nine-rung ladder, each rung a symbol of one of the levels of the heavenly upper world, and a place to which the shaman's soul "journeys" (Harner 2013) in trance (Peters 1982, 1998).

Furthermore, there is a major pan-Himalayan, pre-Buddhist mythos that is well known in almost all the Himalayan cultures (Nepal, Tibet, Bhutan, etc.), among Buddhist and Hindu alike, and that is the stories about the *yeti*. In a pivotal chapter, different sizes and types of yeti are identified, one of which is a child abductor and, at the same time, master shaman teacher and initiator of future shamans. That is to say, some of the tales of the yeti have a role in the shamanic ecstatic experience.

REFERENCES

Bellezza, J. V. *Spirit Mediums, Sacred Mountains and Related Bön Textual Traditions in Upper Tibet.* Boston: Brill, 2005.

Berglie, P. A. "Preliminary Remarks on Some Tibetan 'Spirit Mediums' in Nepal." *Kailash* 4, no. 1 (1976): 85–108.

———. "Tibetan Spirit-Mediumship: Change and Continuity." In *Tibetan Studies: Proceedings of the 5th Seminar of the International Association for Tibetan Studies,* Vol. 2, edited by S. Ihara and Z. Yamaguchi, 361–368. Tokyo: Narita, 1992.

Harner, M. *Cave and Cosmos: Shamanic Encounters with Another Reality.* Berkeley, CA: North Atlantic Books, 2013.

Kingsley, P. *A Story Waiting to Pierce You: Mongolia, Tibet and the Destiny of the Western World.* Point Reyes, CA: Golden Sufi Center, 2010.

Peters, L. "Trance, Initiation, and Psychotherapy in Tamang Shamanism." *American Ethnologist* 9, no. 1 (1982): 21–46.

———. *Tamang Shamans.* New Delhi: Nirala Books, 1998.

Samuel, G. *Civilized Shamans.* Washington, DC: Smithsonian Institution Press, 1993.

·1·

TRADITION, PRACTICE, *and* TRANCE[2]

This chapter is the result of ethnographic research on Tibetan shamanism as practiced at Tashi Palkhiel, a refugee camp established for Tibetans who fled Tibet after the Chinese invasion of 1959, a few miles from Pokhara, Nepal. Its focus is the two shamans currently residing there, and a third who recently died, their healing practices, their trance, their beliefs about the soul, as well as their status and role as shamans in the culture of a refugee camp. The research presented here has yielded new data that demands a reassessment of the well-documented "soul calling—life calling" ritual, as well as of the distinctive type of journeying and possession-trance of the so-called Tibetan "spirit medium."

Tashi Palkhiel is the largest of three refugee camps in the area, and has a population of about 1,400. Currently there are no shamans practicing at the other two camps. I have known the late Pau (shaman)[3] Karma Wangchuk and Pau Nyima Dhondup (sixty-eight years old) since 1996, and met Pau Rhichoe[4] (seventy-one years old) in 1998. Pau Wangchuk was the first FSS (Foundation for Shamanic Studies) "Living Treasure" and Pau Nyima and Pau Rhichoe two of its most recent. Each year, I have spent about two weeks with the pau with members of my educational groups, observing their rituals and conducting interviews. In 2008, ethnographic fieldwork covered a period of three months. Wangchuk died prior to this latest research effort. Over the years I've witnessed more than a hundred of the pau's healing rituals.

The shamanism of the three camp pau has been the subject of ethnographic research for nearly thirty-five years. Per-Arne Berglie's (1976, 1978, 1982, 1983, 1992) landmark studies described the "séances," trances, and cultural context of the camp pau. Years later, Sarah Sifers (2005), a field associate for FSS, describes, and in her 2008 film depicts, the practice of the pau, including elements of the "soul calling—life calling" ritual (*la kuk tshé kuk* [*bla hgugs tshe hgugs*]) commonly called *la kuk*. There has been greater focus on Wangchuk, who achieved some notoriety. Bellezza (2005, 66ff.), based on his interviews in 1998 with Wangchuk, identifies him as a knowledgeable representative of the Tibetan spirit-medium tradition. A short narrative appeared in Dunham and Baker (1993), a text with a foreword by H.H. the Dalai Lama. Wangchuk became a "Living Treasure" after being nominated by Ian Baker, a longtime FSS Nepal field associate (Baker 1991), and a few short "status reports" appeared in FSS journals (Peters 1997a, 2008; Sifers 2007; Sifers and Peters 2001). Having research spanning many years on the same shamans at the same location makes it possible to discern the effects of cultural change and deepen understanding.

SHAMAN, *LAMA,* AND BÖN

The pau are Buddhist but their shamanic practice and beliefs originated in the Tibetan indigenous tradition known as Bön.[5] Tibetologists distinguish an old form of Bön that has an oral tradition, and a later form that has a literary tradition and is monastic like Buddhism and arose after Buddhism came to Tibet. These two forms are sometimes referred to as "revealed Bön" and the newer systematized development "textual Bön." The latter is a religious order but, in the earlier tradition, Bön or Bön *po* (practitioners of Bön) refers to an independent "indigenous priest," "invoker," "sorcerer," or, more to the point, "shaman," and does not refer to a church or organized religion (Hoffmann 1961, 13ff.,

98–99; Li 1948, 33–36; Snellgrove and Richardson 1968, 59, 96–103; Stein 1972, 232–235). The earlier Bön is the indigenous shamanic tradition prior to the arrival from India of Padma Sambhava, the Buddhist cultural hero who is credited with bringing Buddhism to Tibet in 749 CE, subduing the local Bön deities, converting them to Buddhism, and binding them by oath to be "defenders of the Buddhist faith" (*dharmapala* in Sanskrit, *sung mo* [*srung mo*]) (Nebesky-Wojkowitz 1993, 3ff.). It is these converted Bön deities, the dharmapala, and not the heavenly high-ranking Buddhist deities (*lha*), who have the significant role in the Tibetan shamanism practiced at the camp.

The camp pau do not affirm affiliation to Bön, as Bön is heresy to Buddhism. They trace their origin as shamans to Padma Sambhava in the eighth century, and not to Bön. Nevertheless, the practice of shamanism is not part of the Buddhist structure and reflects beliefs and an indigenous tradition (revealed Bön) prior to Buddhist cultural patrimony (Bellezza 2005, 2). It is part of what Tucci (1988, 163ff.) calls the prehistoric Tibetan "folk religion." In other words, shamanism is an extant traditional sacred profession in a culture dominated by Buddhism for more than a millennium.

Buddhist preeminence and the hierarchy of lama[6] and shaman are formally validated in a myth that, in one version or another, is omnipresent in Tibetan culture. Moreover, this key story is represented on the shaman's altar (see Figure 1-1). To the far left and far right of the pau's altar sit two cone-shaped piles of *tsampa* [*rtsam pa*] (roasted barley flour) with a pile of rice in the center. Each is placed on its own raised round wooden tray. The pile on the right in Figure 1-1 is Mt. Kailash (Tee Tsee [Ti Rtse]), the holy Hindu and Buddhist mountain thought to be at the center of the world, and an axis linking heaven and earth. Originally, Tee Tsee was a mountain sacred to the Bön. Historical texts characterize it as a Bön *ri* or "Bön mountain" (Tucci 1988, 219) and the surrounding area, a famed center of Bön activity (Hoffmann 1961, 98–99). In the story, as told by Pau Nyima:

> Milarepa, the Buddhist ascetic saint, and the Bön shaman, Naro Bön Jung, had a contest to race up to the top of Kailash. The one who reached the peak first would win jurisdiction over the mountain and religious authority.
>
> Naro raced up by playing his drum, the sound of the drum being his horse.
>
> Meanwhile, Milarepa remained asleep. When his assistant came to awaken him, Milarepa said, "Call me when the sun rises." Later, he flew on a rainbow to the peak and, on his way past Naro, Naro fell to the ground along with his drum, landing upon stinging nettles, a food sacred to Milarepa but that stung the shaman.[7] The dark, descending ravines on one side of the mountain show the path of Naro's fall. However, Milarepa felt compassion for the shaman and gave him, as consolation, a less important mountain (Tee Jung [Ti Cung]), depicted on the left of the altar), where Naro resides with his drum.[8]

Although this story is about the eclipse of Bön, it also affirms an enduring but marginalized and circumscribed role in religious culture, a "small portion," Nyima says—the less holy mountain where the shaman resides with his drum—graciously given to the defeated shaman by the Buddhist saint. Thus this myth, which explains elements present on the altar, provides a cultural charter for the persistence of traditional shamanism—that is, the practice of the pau.

At the camp, the pau's practice is independent of the Buddhist lama, but the lama grant authority by recognition. A lama sometimes presents the pau the fabric from which his first costume will be sewn. Nyima received such material from a *rinpoché* (priest of high rank and education) of the Sakya lineage. H. H. the Dalai Lama gave Wangchuk an old and tattered costume once belonging to the State Oracle as well as a letter certifying the authenticity of his work after he was called to Dharamsala (the residence in exile of H. H. the Dalai Lama) to do healings.[9] All of the pau's ritual paraphernalia are consecrated (*rab né* [*rab gnas*]) by lama and therefore sacred (see Figures 1-2 and 1-3). Further, much of it is gifted by lama. The pau take pilgrimages to many sacred Buddhist sites, monasteries, and teachers seeking power, knowledge, and blessing.

The pau are tested by respected lama, as well as by "elder pau," which is how Rhichoe referred to his teachers in Tibet. Testing discerns if a candidate has visions of deities or demons in a brass mirror (*ling* [*gling*]). This is done to determine whether his strange behavior is the result of a "calling" by the deities to shamanism or an illness caused by harmful spirits (*né pa* [*gnöd pa*]). The former initiates shamanic training; the latter necessitates healing by pau or by lama.

Nyima told Berglie (1976, 93) a pau needed knowledge in four subjects: (1) the channels or veins (*tsa* [*rtsa*]) in the body; (2) how to describe the appearance of the gods seen in the brass mirror, as occurs in testing. A lama or elder pau teaches these first two subjects. A pau must also know: (3) how to heal by sucking (*jib* [*hjib*]);[10] and (4) how to invoke the proper deities to do jib and other ritual healing procedures. These last two must be learned from another pau.

The pau often refer their patients for supplemental healing by a camp lama. These lama are distinct from the rinpoché and monks who reside in Jangchub Choeling, the large camp monastery of the Kagyüdpa order that has about 120 resident monks and a Buddhist educational institute. The lama to whom the pau refer are lay lama who, while robed, reside in the camp with their families. A pau, after healing a patient, may decide the patient also needs a long life empowerment (*tshé wang* [*tshe dbang*]), or may ask a camp lama to read from the holy texts (*ngak* [*sngags*]), parts of which contain powerful *mantra* and spells necessary to strengthen a person. Although they have overlapping responsibilities, and perform some rituals with the same purpose, the pau do them in a way distinct from these lama. There is also a *ngak pa* [*sngags pa*] at the camp. Ngak pa are thought to be "half-shaman" and "half-lama." The current ngak pa does little work on his own and often participates with the camp lama in their healings.

The pau say that their rituals are "wild," and this primarily distinguishes them from those of lama and ngak pa, who, by contrast, chant from their holy books and sit peacefully. The pau are wild because they enter trance by simultaneously and loudly playing a small two-sided, hourglass-shaped *dharu*[11] (hand drum) and *shang* [*gshang*] (flat bell), one in each hand, sometimes for an hour or longer; dance; channel deities and ferocious animals; suck illness from the patient, often swallowing the polluted substance after extracting it; and demonstrate mastery over fire by handling live coals.

Dramatically, healing feathers from the divine *thang kar* (lammergeier) sometimes fell from the ceiling of Wangchuk's house after it was invoked. When the deities arrive at the ritual, some come on horseback. Nyima sits with bent knees and bounces as if astride a horse. He often whinnies. When the deities dismount, they dance and then jump upon their seats. Deity-embodied Rhichoe once broke the heavy wooden frame of a patient's bed. Further, they wear multicolored silk embroidered costumes with a five-pointed crown (*ringa* [*rigs lnga*]) when embodied.

Possession-trance and spirit mediumship, the latter involving verbal communication, are the most salient characteristics of the pau's dramatic healing rituals. During these altered consciousness states, the countenance of the pau changes, taking on the wrathful appearance of their deity and speaking with a commanding voice, impatiently demanding obedience, sometimes hurling insults at those present.

Although it is necessary to invoke the deity for healing, it is also important not to irritate him, as he can be irascible and may decide not to do the healing. Thus, neither the patient nor spectators interact directly with the deity. There is an "intermediary" or "intercessor" (*bar mee* [*bar mi*]) who has been trained by a pau to appropriately honor and speak to the deity and to relay the deity's message to the patient during ritual.

The dramatic practices of the pau have survived from pre-Buddhist times when most Tibetans were rugged nomadic herders, and being "wild," "tough," and "untamed" was prized as a cultural value, and shamanism was dominant, unlike the agricultural, urban, and sedentary life-way of Buddhism in Tibet (see Ekvall 1968, 92–93; Samuel 1993, 218, 222). In fact, shamanism is an integral part of the pastoral community in Tibet and has persisted even into current times in nomadic settlements of upper Tibet, far from urban centers, despite fifty years of communism (Bellezza 2005, 4–5, 8–9). Although they are from different settlements in Tibet, the camp pau were all engaged in animal husbandry and trade before the exile, like other Tibetan herders. In their practice, there are many surviving elements of that life-way. For example, the pau are responsible for the treatment of cattle and other livestock, although there is hardly any need at the camp.

I asked the pau, who are committed Buddhists, how they integrate two contrary systems: one (shamanic) that recognizes the reality of soul and spirit, and the other (Buddhist), which does not. When they couldn't explain, I followed their advice and consulted Khedup Rinpoche, who spends several months each year teaching at the camp's Buddhist educational institute. He likened the two systems to the differences between the "ultimate" and the "relative" aspects of reality. The relative speaks to the beliefs and customs of the people, including the animistic "folk religion" that gives context to shamanic healing. Ultimately, these beliefs are not real. Still, illness and healing are manifestly real. Therefore, the Buddha adjusted his methods to include the practices of the people. With this argument, the rinpoché seemed to acknowledge the pragmatic aspects of the pau's healing work while at the same time undermining its spiritual foundations. Thus shamanism and Buddhism coexist in the refugee camp.

THE *LA* AND *SAUG* SOULS AND THE "SOUL CALLING" RITUAL

The pau maintain that there is only one soul, the *nam shé* [*nam çes*]. As a Buddhist concept, the nam shé is consciousness in a very wide sense; it has a number of constituent parts, including the *la* [*bla*] and *saug* [*srog*], but is not conceived as a soul. Still, because the nam shé is immortal, the pau liken it to the *atma* (Sanskrit) of Hinduism; that is to say, they see it as a soul. Thus the la and the saug would appear to be soul parts, but this is difficult to state definitively.

In describing their experiences, the pau sometimes miss the terminological precision of the rinpoché, because they have not had a Buddhist education nor are they literate. Their knowledge comes from tutelage, not from books. For example, they often use the terms la and nam shé interchangeably. In so doing, the pau convey the notion that the la, like the nam shé, is consciousness, which is similar to the belief of other Tibetan shamans. Based on his interviews in Tibet and with shamans in exile, Bellezza (2005, 7) writes that the shamans believe that their "consciousness principle" is the la. Pau Nyima says, "The la is the spirit inside the person" (Sifers 2005, 114). Therefore, the la has an ontology or beingness and is not merely the impersonal psychological function or principle of consciousness, but the spirit of consciousness. The la also has the attributes of *sem* [*sems*] (mind and thinking) and *rig pa* (reasoning and intelligence). The la soul, it seems, is that spirit that constitutes a person, a conscious thinking being.

The pau say that the la possesses *nu shug* [*nus shugs*]—that is, power, force, energy, and strength—and liken it to the Indian concept of *shakti* (albeit without the goddess identity). It is the power of nu shug that "animates" the body (see Bellezza 2005, 93). When a person dies, the la leaves the body; the body then becomes a corpse because there is no nu shug to animate physical existence. Nu shug also relates to personal power, skills, talent, strengths, and magical and shamanic abilities. It is also a cosmic power possessed by deities and the inherent power found in sacred objects and amulets. Nu shug is ardor and passion, as well as capability. A diminishment of nu shug is a weakening of the la, and a concomitant loss of physical strength, personal power, health, passion, motivation, mental acuity, and focus; even a person's luck is diminished.

Bön shamans, like the pau themselves, speak of two souls or soul parts, the *la* and the *saug* or *tshé*.[12] As the full name of the "soul calling" ritual indicates, la kuk tshé kuk, the two souls are interrelated and figure in the healing. *Saug* means life and is also the "breath soul." It is inseparable from the body. It flows in the breath, has its seat in the heart, but penetrates throughout the body. It is the life-force spirit within us that opposes death and, after death, seeks rebirth. When it is weakened, our resistance to death is weakened, and consequently, our life is shortened (Nebesky-Wojkowitz 1993, 493; Baumer 2002, 49–50; Stein 1972, 232; Tucci 1988, 192–193). Here too the weakness of the soul is the result of a loss of nu shug, which supplies vital energy to the saug.

Pre-Buddhist Bön defines the la as a "shadow soul," a living double that can temporarily leave the body and wander about; such a "free soul" may thus find itself vulnerable to attack and capture (Baumer 2002, 49–50; Tucci 1988, 192–193). Further, researchers generally agree that a lost or wandering soul (la) is "called back" or "returned" by a pau or lama performing the important la kuk (soul calling) ritual (Berglie 1983, 164; Lessing 1951, 265; Sifers 2005, 117–118; 2008; Tucci 1988, 190f.). Berglie and Sifers describe material gathered at the camp from the same shamans as myself; Lessing and Tucci rely on archival Lamaist texts. However, contrary to my current research, the pau at the camp fundamentally disagree with the definition of the la as a free soul and instead view it as bound to the body in both sickness and health.

I will return to explain this discrepancy shortly. It leads to a new interpretation of the ritual and means of accounting for its efficacy. First, for clarity, dominant aspects of the ritual will be described.

To do la kuk, the pau have three methods: one using a slingshot, another floating a cup in a tub of water, and the third utilizing black and white stones. In all methods, three kinds of beads typically worn as a part of a necklace by Tibetans—one representing the patient's bones (made of conch), another symbolizing blood (coral), and the third (turquoise) the brilliant or glowing appearance of a fully healthy person (*dang* [*mdangs*])—are brought to the ritual by the patient (see Figure 1-4). The beads are pressed into an image of a sheep (*la lug* [*bla lug*] or "soul sheep") made of *spag* [*spags*] (roasted barley flour dough) in the first two methods.

In the first method of *la kuk,* which I did not witness but which Pau Nyima explained, a large pot or tub of milky water, likened to Lake Manasarovar, the sacred lake below Mt. Kailash, is covered with a silk greeting scarf (*khatak* [*kha btags*]).[13] The spag image containing the beads is placed into a slingshot and taken outside by an assistant and flung as far as possible. The cloth is then removed from the top of the tub of water and, if the turquoise and the other beads are found in the holy water still spotted with spag and debris from where it was thrown, the soul was successfully called. Afterward the patient cleanses with the holy water, and the beads are worn as an amulet.

In the second method, the beads and spag sheep (la lug) are put into a cup, which is floated in the tub of holy water. The cup is spun and, if the spag sheep faces the patient when it stops moving, it indicates success. This is determined by stretching a khatak scarf from the far end of the pot, and across the water to the patient. Thus the direction of the la lug can be precisely determined when it stops turning.

I observed Pau Nyima use yet another method when there were two patients who both required la kuk. For one patient, the cup stopped moving and the sheep faced the patient. For the other client, when the sheep did not face her, nine white and nine black stones were placed in the tub of milky water and the patient was asked to pick three stones. If, on three choices, a patient picks a majority of white stones, a successful calling of the soul is said to have occurred, albeit even one black stone might require supplemental strengthening of the la by a camp lama. Less than two white stones, similar to failure in the other two methods, demands another la kuk, usually after the patient receives a lama empowerment (*wang*) or ritual reading from the sacred texts (ngak). La kuk ends by the patient cleansing with the water and wearing the amulet, as in the first two methods.

The tub of water and one of the barley flour mounds on the altar (Lake Manasarovar and Mt. Kailash) are linked not only in geographic proximity, but in mythology. They are the "mother" and "father" of the region respectively and, in Buddhist philosophy, which is superimposed on the myth, both lake and mountain together are necessary for liberation (Tucci 1988, 219–220). Mt. Kailash is a *la ree* [*bla ri*] (soul mountain) said, in western Tibet, to be in sympathetic connection with the soul of the country (See Figure 1-5). Similarly, Lake Manasarovar (which means "mind lake" in Sanskrit) is a soul lake (*la tsho* [*bla mtsho*]) where pilgrims bathe to purify soul and mind and seek healing (Ermakov 2008, 17). In the ritual room, Mt. Kailash is, as mentioned above, prominently represented on the altar. The tub of water is a few feet away and below the pau's altar. The lake and mountain set the stage for the ritual. Pau Rhichoe says the altar and the ritual area should be made as if it were a holy place of pilgrimage. Thus, the ritual is a symbolic pilgrimage to the sacred mountain and lake; that is, to the mythical center of the world for healing and purification.

What surprises me is that both pau emphatically state that the la is not a wandering free soul; that, when a person is alive, the la can't leave the body without causing immediate death. If the la leaves, a person will fall to the ground and not have the energy (nu shug) to maintain consciousness or to animate his body, nor would his vital organs continue to function. Thus he will quickly die.

I protested to Pau Nyima that, in order to be called back, as in the la kuk tshé kuk ceremony, the la would first need to leave the body and, while it is true that a person may be seriously ill and eventually die, death did not seem impending in the cases I observed. I reminded him that, although the patients for whom I saw him do la kuk were distressed, they were awake and conscious. In response to these questions and statements, Nyima got up, threw his hands up, slapped them against his sides, obviously frustrated, and complained that I didn't understand the soul. He left the house and took a ten-minute break, leaving Migmar and me in utter confusion. So I decided to approach the subject from another angle.

When he returned, I asked him what term he used for "soul loss." There followed a ten-minute discussion with Migmar, which I didn't understand. It seemed that the conversation was going nowhere. Nyima and Migmar also speak Nepali, so I asked them again, using the term Nepalese shamans use for soul loss. After a long pause, Migmar said, "There is no such idea. The pau do la kuk tshé kuk because the patient's la has been damaged and is deteriorating." Later, Nyima used more descriptive terms for the symptoms like weak, dizzy, and lazy.

I also discussed this with Rhichoe, who added to Nyima's list, saying it was similar to when "cattle are scattered in every direction." The person is confused and cannot think clearly. When he is at home, he wants to leave, and when he is out he wants to return. This fragmentation of consciousness and other symptoms are understood as a weakening of the soul, which the pau call *la nyam* [*bla nyams*]. In la nyam, the mind is weak. The person is unable to focus his thoughts. His soul is being "pushed down" and therefore has lost its clarity and vitality. The person looks dull, his skin has no luster or glow, his eyes have no sparkle or light; even if he dresses well and is clean, he does not look fresh. He has no appetite but, if he eats, he gets no energy from the food. The cause of these oppressive symptoms is always a frightening experience, possibly from a nightmare or a physical trauma or by having been scared by a ghost, leading to the diminishment of nu shug and thus of the la and of the life force (saug), which is the disorder known as la nyam. If not treated, la nyam will in time cause death.

Now, at root the problem is the client's relationship to certain spirits that cause him to become vulnerable. According to Rhichoe, the *zhee dak* [*gshi bdag*], earth deities who rule lakes and rivers, bridges and roads, but mostly mountains, or the *yul lha* "country gods" (local protector deities of villages, valleys, meadows, etc.), have been offended due to the client's nonobservant, careless, i.e., "defiling," actions (*dip* [*grib*]). It is these deities that attack the client, making him susceptible to la nyam. The pau speaks to them on behalf of the client, says mantra, and plays the drum; and his intermediary (bar mee) makes offerings of water in every direction from the tall vessel (*bum pa*) on the altar, with the ritual spoon lying across it, all in order to dissuade them from causing further harm. The rice sprinkled on the red altar cloth is also an offering to them and other low-ranking deities and nefarious spirits that might be present at the ritual.

It is because of la nyam that pau do la kuk. The pau need to "bring up" the la, to strengthen it and restore its brilliance. It is "deteriorating" and "degenerating," so you need to "rise it up." I asked Rhichoe what he means by "rise it up." He replied, "When you add water to a vessel, the floating things rise up," referring to la kuk as, when the pau add sacred water to the tub, it simultaneously turns and gives rise to the cup holding the sheep and the beads. Nyima said, "Nothing is brought back, but grown." The nu shug and the attractiveness and glow of health (dang) are restored and increased. Nyima typically uses the common term *lang wa* to express "to rise." When I asked if there was a more technical shamanic term, he gave a penetrating look like a teacher to a student who must not have been paying attention and emphatically said, "la kuk." Thus the soul (la) is raised up, not summoned back, in the "soul calling" ritual. In other words, a person can lose his power and consequently his health due to a fright, but not his soul.

In my previous research with the pau, I had harbored the assumption of a free la soul (Peters 2004, 132–133). On numerous occasions, my translator had interpreted that Nyima, while in trance, had seen his deities in the mirror (ling) find a patient's soul. Sifers (2005, 118) relates that the deities search for the la and, if retrieved, the sheep effigy will face the patient and stop turning in the water. Berglie (1983, 164) writes, "... man can lose his 'soul' for many reasons. Demons may ... steal it and carry it away ... The aim of the la kuk ritual is then to locate the lost la and bring it back to its owner." This research is completely at odds with what I have reported above. Thus, I endeavored to make sure, with both Nyima and Rhichoe, that nothing was lost in translation this time. I brought the topic up continually and even drew pictures depicting the la departing the body, which they both explicitly stated was impossible.

This, however, does not explain the statement of such a thorough scholar as Berglie. It is to Berglie's (1983, 163) credit that he forthrightly states his information is only "fragmentary" as regards la kuk. He did not witness the ritual, "met" only one case (1976, 99), and did not give a Tibetan term for "soul loss," whereas for almost every other important aspect of camp shamanism, the native term was dutifully recorded.

Sifers and I use the same translator. For over a decade, Migmar and I misconstrued the loss of the soul's power (la nyam) for soul loss. The dictionary definition of *kuk* is a good indicator of why there has been confusion and mistranslation. It does have the meaning mentioned above, "to bring back" and "to return," but this does not necessarily mean to call back or return an entity that has left the physical body. To restore power, strength, glow, etc., to the body-bound soul is just as likely an interpretation as is the presumption of an errant soul. Kuk also means "to turn on, activate, assemble, enrich, make shiny, conjure up, and stir up" and, as Nyima maintains, "to rise," all of which fit the ritual purpose, being remedial for la nyam (see Goldstein 2001, 238; Das 1974, 288).

My current findings are, of course, limited to the pau at the camp. There are recent ethnographic reports of Tibetan shamans residing in exile, and others from upper Tibet, who send their deities to search for a patient's soul (la) that has strayed and, when found, the deities do a "soul retrieval" as part of the la kuk ceremony (Bellezza 2005, 33, 132–133). Furthermore, summoning back a wandering soul is an old and frequent ritual theme in both Bön and early Lamaism (Karmay 1998, 310ff.), as is the motif that the souls (la and saug) can be damaged and weakened (Ermakov 2008, 524).[14]

Lessing (1951, 263) published an analysis of a tract from a Lamaist text entitled "Ritual for calling the soul and for calling life," i.e., la kuk tshé kuk. It is identified as a "life prolonging ritual." The text was from the thirteenth century, but the practice described came from an earlier time. From the tract, it can be discerned that the ritual attempts to achieve its purpose of life prolongation by raising the patient's life force that is deteriorating or declining, as well as to return to the patient a lost soul. Portions read:

Be pleased to accept these
substitutions
Release what ye hold and loosen
what is tied
Release what is captured and
raise what is downtrodden …
What is declining is being
fortified; what was broken is
continued …
Whether thou art snatched away
or carried off
I bid thee come back.

(Lessing 1951, 272)

The lama calls back the soul through textual recitations. However, the "soul calling" litany is only one aspect of the Lamaist ritual. The lama uses substitute offerings in the image of the patient (*luh* [*glüd*]), even a sheep's leg (la lug) from an animal that was not intentionally killed as "ransom" for the captured soul (Lessing 1951, 267).[15]

The pau's la kuk, unlike the prescription in the lama text, makes no offerings due to a soul theft. There is no offering, because in la nyam (deterioration of the la) there is no stolen soul to ransom. The central remedial element is the discovery and retrieval of the three stones—turquoise, coral, and shell—in the water in the slingshot method, which will be worn by the patient as an amulet. One of the helpers in the retinue of Nyima's principal spirit, the mountain deity, Thang Lha,[16] is envisioned (*mig pa* [*dmig pa*]) in a mirror on the altar to find the three stones and bring them to the holy water (see Figure 1-6). The way is marked by flags of the five different primary colors, symbolizing the five directions, five elements, and the five Wisdom Buddhas, antidotes for the five poisons that plague mind and body, that are placed around Lake Manasarovar (the pot of water).

In the second method, the sheep (la lug), one of Thang Lha's helpers, is charged to protect and to carry the three stones containing the power that will heal the soul and the body and to "supervise" that the la kuk is done appropriately and, if so, will turn to face the patient in the holy water, aligning itself with the outstretched scarf. In Sifers's (2008) film, once it was determined that the sheep faced toward the patient, one end of the silk khatak was momentarily placed on the sheep, and the other end touched by the patient to his forehead. Thus, the scarf with its interwoven signs of good fortune provides a bridge for the passage or "translation" (*gyur wa* [*hgyur ba* or *sgyur ba*]) of nu shug healing power from the sheep and stones to the patient. Final healing elements might include the patient wearing new clothes, or being given a new name, but it is necessary to wear the amulet and cleanse with the holy water.

I discussed with the pau the often stated but inaccurate belief that the la can take up residence in a number of objects outside of the body, like trees, lakes, mountains, and animals, as well as in a valued turquoise (see Figure 1-7). Such a stone is called a "soul turquoise" (*la yu* [*bla gyu*]) and is sometimes considered to be the dwelling place of a person's soul (*la né* [*bla gnas*]). Of course, Nyima knew of the "soul turquoise" because it is the name of the stone utilized in la kuk, but this did not mean to him that the la could ever be located there or anywhere else outside the body.

Figure 1-7. Pau Richoe and Larry Peters. Photo by Carol Peters.

Nyima would agree with Ermakov (2008, 519–520) that la né refers to a very strong connection between a person and an object or another person. So much so that, if one is damaged, the other will also suffer. For example, if a parent has a strong sympathetic connection to his child, the Tibetans might say that his soul resides (la né) with the child. However, this does not mean that the child possesses the parent's soul. Rather, it refers to a strong emotional bonding and identification, and not the physical location of the la.

It is in this experiential sense of sympathy and merging of identity that the "soul turquoise" and what it represents is connected to the patient and the healing purpose of the ritual. The stone is a symbol of the glow of the healthy person (dang) because it doesn't become dull, never losing its shine. Further, the turquoise is believed to contain the emanations of light of the sun and the moon and thus, when recovered in the holy water, is seen as a gift from the heavenly realm of the gods (lha) that restores light, shine, and the glow of life to the soul and body, reactivating and reinvigorating the powers of the la and saug. Likewise, the coral, symbolic of blood, is seen as a gift of the middle world deities of mountain and red rock (*sten* [*bstan*]); and the shell, symbolic of bone, is believed to be a gift of the *lu* [*klu*], the lower world, earth's bodies of water, and wells, serpent deities. Thus the stones impart a cosmic force and power (nu shug) that brings the patient a strong, healthy glow, blood, and bone.

La kuk is not a soul retrieval; it is a life-extending empowerment, a power (nu shug) raising, restoration, and retrieval. Simply put, it is a ritual to bring power to the la and the saug and thus heal the deteriorating soul and life force. Moreover, it is a method to evoke a transpersonal experience in the patient, a feeling of connection to the cosmos and the deities from which the stones obtain their healing capacity. The stones are empowered by the deities from each of the three worlds and are delivered in the holy water, the symbol of the purifying lake of soul and mind at the earth's central mountain, the axis of ascent and descent of the deities. The stones are then worn by the patient, restoring power to soul (la) and body, and increasing the life force (saug).

Nyima, in Sifers's (2008) film, explains that he tells the patient, at the end of the treatment, to "remember" the deities' healing gifts and to "take refuge" (*gyub dro* [*skyabs hgro*]) in them; that is, to become devoted to them, to pray and meditate for their guidance and protection, and likewise to show compassion and kindness to all beings.

THE *SAUG* AND THE *NAM SHÉ* IN THE SHAMAN'S TRANCE

The Lamaist text is a reflection of how Lamaism integrated numerous Bön and traditional beliefs into its practices and rituals. Samuel (1993, 564) argued that Buddhism was largely successful in Tibet because it was able to incorporate pre-Buddhist shamanism into its practices and literature. However, this assimilation process worked both ways and shamanism has integrated certain Buddhist beliefs and contemplative practices into its system, albeit altered to suit its purposes.

In the system of the pau, the saug is located in the center of the chest, at the place known as the *saug tsa,* the "vein of life" or "root of life." The *tsa* are subtle "veins" or "channels" and the saug tsa is the center where all the channels in the body converge. When the pau enters trance and becomes a spirit medium, all his tsa are filled with the light and radiance (*hé dzer* [*höd gdser*]) of the deity, which emanates from the center of his chest or saug tsa and flows throughout the body. The process of being filled with the light is also called "taking refuge" by the pau, and refuge is the requisite state of consciousness for almost all shamanic healing.[17]

Besides the saug tsa, there is the *uma tsa* [*dbu ma rtsa*], which leads from the top of the head to the center of the chest; that is, to the saug tsa. The other two tsa are the *kyang ma* [*rkyang ma*] or moon channel, which leads from the fourth finger of the right hand, and the *ro ma* or sun channel, which leads from the fourth finger of the left hand to the saug tsa. The deity's radiance enters the body through the tsa openings in the fingers and travels to the uma central channel or vein via the saug tsa and rises up to the head and then reverses its course and goes back down into the saug tsa from which it emanates.[18]

For the pau, taking refuge begins by invoking the deity through visualization (mig pa). During this process, which may last fifteen to twenty minutes or more, the pau rapidly plays his hand drum and bell and invites the deities to come down. Combined with the percussion, Rhichoe's breathing becomes fast and short, almost hyperventilating, for perhaps three or four minutes, which reminds me of a psychotherapeutic and trance-induction method known as "holotropic breathing" (Grof 1985, 387–389). After the deities descend (*lha pab pa* [*lha hbab pa*]), they take their place, according to status, in the proper brass mirror (ling) on the altar. The silk scarf wrapped around the pictures of the deities is the method of respectful greeting.

Traditionally, there are three vertical mirrors placed on the altar, one for each class of deity (upper, middle, and lower worlds) invoked, but one or two mirrors are sufficient according to Rhichoe. When two mirrors are used, the location of the numerous types of middle world deities is in the upper mirror along with the lha (the heavenly gods). The serpentine lu are in the lower mirror (see Figure 1-1). Ling, the term used to identify the mirrors, primarily means "world." Thus the vertical mirrors represent the different worlds and levels of a tripartite cosmos.

According to Pau Rhichoe, whose altar is represented in Figure 1-1, the cone-shaped pile of rice in the center, in between the two mountains, is actually not a mountain but the "environment," "space," or "field" that encompasses the three worlds found in the mirrors. These worlds contain everything that is part of the ordinary external world, as Rhichoe says he can "see" mountains, persons, villages, etc. But he can also see spirits and deities in the mirrors, and his experiences and visions are not bound by ordinary space and time.

The focus is the middle world. All the lesser deities and spirits that attack a patient are middle world except for the serpent lu. Further, the deities the shaman is a medium for, in rituals that I've witnessed, are all powerful middle world mountain deities, typically described to be outfitted with armor, weapons, and victory banners on horseback or bird vehicles, all of whom were once Bön but have been converted to Buddhism (i.e., became dharmapala or sung mo). They have not achieved enlightenment and therefore do not have the status of the heavenly Buddhist deities (lha); consequently, they reside in the middle world. Yet they have taken a vow to be protectors and guardians of the Buddhist faith (Nebesky-Wojkowitz 1993, 3ff.). Thus, while being warriors, they can also be compassionate healers.[19]

The mirror(s) are crucial because, if they are not set up on the altar, the deities will not come. When the deities descend, they take their place according to rank in the "huge halls" that are seen in the mirrors, and the pau are able to describe this in detail. As stated above, the ling is the tool used to test the visions of shaman candidates; and by looking into it, the pau can view the activities they require their deities or their deities' helpers to perform. Nyima compares the mirror to a television and, like Wangchuk, typically wears one around his neck during ritual. With this ling in hand, Nyima would often point it at the patient or others present, to "see" what type of spirit might be causing trouble to them. In this sense, the ling is a window into a "nonordinary reality," but is also a doorway through which the deities enter ritual reality, are channeled by the pau, who take refuge in them, and thus, through the pau, do their healing work.

During the ritual refuge process, according to Rhichoe, the lights reflecting in the altar ling from a candle or the lights in the room become ever larger and brighter, indicating that the deities invoked have descended. Their brilliance fills the room. Then the fiery radiance of Rhichoe's refuge deity (a red sten he calls Sangri Sten, second from the left on the altar) is seen to emerge from the mirror and enter the pau's body through the ro ma tsa and kyang ma tsa; and, when it reaches the saug tsa in the heart, there is a momentary flash of intense heat that causes the pau to shake. Then the deity's fiery radiance continues its course up the uma tsa to the head and down again to the saug tsa, to infuse the entire body through thousands of smaller veins, completing refuge. Pau Rhichoe says, "It's like a cup being filled with tea." When refuge is attained, this is signaled in the ritual by the pau putting on his headdress (ringa) and, soon afterward, the bar mee intermediary will place a khatak in the lobes of the headdress, to honor the deity's arrival.

The schematic of subtle channels has obvious parallels to both Tibetan Buddhist meditation and medical systems (see Govinda 1960; Dummer 1988). However, there are elements distinct to the pau's manner of taking refuge; for example, the entry point into the pau's body of the deity's radiance at the finger openings of the kyang ma tsa and ro ma tsa. When the pau receives training, his fourth fingers are tied with cloth or string to prevent a deity's radiance from entering the body, and untied gradually and for longer periods of time until the candidate learns to intentionally "open" his tsa in order to receive the radiance. Before completing his training, Nyima could embody the deity's radiance at inappropriate times. Consequently, his fingers were tied if he was attending another pau's healings.[20] However, the fingers are also an exit place for nefarious possessing spirits. For example, in healing rituals involving depossession, the pau will tie the same fingers of the patient to prevent the possessing spirit from leaving the patient's body until the pau has identified it and gotten a promise from it to leave the patient permanently. Then the fingers are untied so the spirit can depart the patient and then is chased away with fiery hot coals.

At the time of refuge, the nam shé[21] or consciousness of the pau is "transformed" (gyur wa) into that of the deity through an exchange process, as Wangchuk and Nyima explain it. Nyima says at first he visualizes (mig pa) his nam shé (soul) leaving his body from the uma tsa at the top of the head at the place of the fontanel and simultaneously the deity's radiant consciousness (nam shé) comes to occupy his body through the kyang ma and ro ma tsa openings at the fourth fingers of each hand.

It is important to point out that the pau distinguish possession (*jug pa* [*hjug pa*]) from refuge. As Rhichoe summed it up while pointing to a light bulb hanging from the ceiling, "The pau become the light, not the bulb. The lights are the emanations (*tulpa* [*sprul pa*]) of the deity." The emanations reflect the consciousness attributes, qualities, and powers of the deity. Therefore, Nyima says it is an exchange of nam shé, albeit with the caveat that the nam shé sent by the deity is not the deity's consciousness as such, but its radiant emanation. Thus the pau becomes an emanation of the deity, not the deity, whose location during refuge is in its appropriate ling. At the same time that the pau receives the radiance of the refuge deity, his nam shé enters into the mirror of his protective deity. Pau Nyima's nam shé is protected by five *khadoma* [*mkhah hgro ma*] goddesses (*dakhini* in Sanskrit). Pau Wangchuk was protected by Padma Sambhava (see Berglie 1976, 99).

As mentioned, the deities' radiance enters the body through the ro ma and kyang ma. To end the trance, it will later exit from these same channels (tsa). The pau's nam shé exits and later returns through the top of the head (uma tsa). Nyima says the exchange in both directions must be simultaneous as it is very dangerous for the pau. Any delays in the exchange could be fatal, as it would be tantamount to a soul loss. Harmful spirits (né pa) are always present during healings and desire to create obstacles, ruin the ritual, cause more pain and suffering to the client, or even enter the pau's body through an open tsa, which is why various deities surround the body and are stationed at each of the tsa openings. The heavenly lha guard the uma; the middle world sten guard the ro ma; the lu guard the kyang ma tsa (Berglie 1982, 152–153).

After taking refuge, the pau come to embody not only the attributes and powers of the deity, but also those of the deity's entire retinue of spirits that descend (*pab pa*) in the deity's emanations. For example, when the pau do jib, they embody the zoomorphic radiance of one of the deity's sucking spirits, typically a mythical dog, wolf, or divine bird with expert extraction power. Wangchuk was able to do "healings at a distance" by sending an avian emanation of the deity across the ocean. Whenever necessary, the refuge deity can send a spirit emanation to do a healing or, as in la kuk, the deity or one of his retinue can "journey" to locate the three slingshotted stones and retrieve them in order to be recovered in the holy water. Thus, the pau do not make a soul journey themselves, but there are situations in which a deity or a member of that deity's entourage makes the journey. These are visionary journeys as the pau witnesses everything in the ling.

At the time of refuge, Nyima and Wangchuk say that, because their nam shé or consciousness is in the mirror, and they are filled with the radiance, they do not remember what they do or say. The loss of memory during mediumship is a widely held view in Tibetan culture, amnesia being the sign of trance authenticity. However, it is obvious from the above that the pau are perfectly able to discuss their trance experiences in detail. On many occasions, after a treatment, Nyima even corrected his intermediary about what the deity said during the ritual, seemingly escaping his attention that such detail betrayed conscious knowledge.

Pau Rhichoe, unlike his colleague pau at the camp, and the late Wangchuk, does not do the consciousness exchange. Rhichoe invokes his deities in the mirror, similar to the others. The deities' lights enter his body in a parallel manner and he performs la kuk, jib, and other rituals like the other pau. There is also no difference in his understanding of the tsa system. The only difference is that his nam shé does not relocate to the ling. Nyima is very critical of this; he says that, without the exchange, there are two consciousnesses in one body simultaneously, the pau's and the deity's. Thus the pau is "half-god, half-man," a consciousness state unsuitable for healing work. For Rhichoe, this is not an issue. He says that self-consciousness is eradicated by the deity's fiery radiance in the refuge process. This accounts for his "amnesia."

I am not sure if Rhichoe represents a different shamanic tradition than the other pau. The pau say that originally there were four types of pau sent to Tibet from the four cardinal directions by Padma Sambhava, all doing a distinct type of healing work to which the pau owe their origin as shamans. However, neither pau is able to identify all these types nor reach agreement on specifics. One type Nyima mentioned is called a *ché pa* [*gcöd pa*]. At one meeting, Rhichoe said he was a ché pa but, at our very next meeting, was quick to correct himself and told me actually he wasn't because only lama are ché pa, and that there are ché pa lama texts. The work he does is similar, he says, but he learned it from his pau teacher in Tibet and not from a lama. Indeed, there are lama texts that explain *ché* as a type of contemplative practice very similar to what Rhichoe does, albeit the shamanic purpose, which is healing, and the Buddhist practice have different objectives (see Evans-Wentz 1958; Nebesky-Wojkowitz 1955, 227–228). Ché is mastered through an initiation that is done numerous times, most often at places where the dead are disposed.[22] Once mastered, ché is employed in most healing rituals by the initiated pau.

Ché means to "cut off." In this work, Rhichoe visualizes the sacrifice of his body, his blood, flesh, and bone to the harmful spirits present during the healing who have come to obstruct the treatment and ultimately cause death. Rhichoe confronts these "graveyard ghosts" whom he calls *pret* (Sanskrit for "hungry ghost"), or less often, *yee dzik* [*yi dsigs*], horrible beings with huge bellies that cause all sorts of illnesses, even epidemics. To these harmful ghosts, Rhichoe promises his body as a substitute for the patient, in order to satiate them. At the same time, he gets the pret to convert and commit to oath that they will be protectors of Buddhism on the model of Padma Sambhava. He says they come with the tools necessary for butchering. Rhichoe sees the sacrifice as an act of compassion and compares it to a story of the

Buddha, who, in one incarnation, likewise sacrificed his body to feed an emaciated tigress and her starving cub (a story found in the Jatakas tales). Ché is done after the deities have descended but prior to refuge. Rhichoe is protected by these deities and by others that control the situation and ensure that nothing goes wrong.

After the sacrifice, Rhichoe says his body comes back together: bones, blood, flesh, with la, saug, and nam shé, which were not sacrificed. If not, he would die, as the la, saug, and nam shé would not have a body. He would not be specific exactly how the "rememberment" occurs, it being too sacred to discuss. He would only say it is quick and spontaneous, and that it produced a change in consciousness (gyur wa) in which all his tsa become "open" to receive the deity's radiance (i.e., to take refuge). At the end of one visit, he gifted me a small carpet with a design of the lotus, and told me to practice ché sitting on it. Days before, he had recounted a well-known story of Padma Sambhava, whose name means "lotus born," that relates the Buddhist hero's death and miraculous rebirth from a lotus in the center of a lake (see Evans-Wentz 1954, 145f.). I cannot explain it, but I know the gift was also a teaching.

Ché has its origins in prehistory. As Eliade (1964, 13–14, 436–437) has articulated, a similar content to ché is found in shamanic initiations across the world. This type of initiation, in which the neophyte witnesses his own death and his flesh being removed from his body ("skeletonized") before he is reconstituted or reborn with a new body and supernatural abilities, may have two causes: (1) the result of a "spontaneous election," i.e., "calling" to shamanism through a vision or dream; or (2) learned from teachers and mastered through contemplative ritual practices. For Rhichoe, it was a series of such initiatory rituals that formed the model for his type of healing practice. This does not mean that he or the other pau did not have spontaneous callings. In fact, each did. However, their callings did not have the same sacrificial content as the initiation to do ché that Rhichoe received from his elder pau teacher.

Earlier it was stated that Tibetan "spirit mediums" meet the criteria for shamanic trance. The generally accepted cross-cultural definition of "ecstasy" or the "shamanic state of consciousness" is fundamentally the "soul journey" (Eliade 1964; Harner 1990). The work of the three pau seems to qualify, as they can direct one of their deities' spirit emanations to make the visionary journey. Thus, even though spirit mediumship and possession-trance are the most dominant aspects of their healings, a spirit journey is part of the pau's repertoire.

THE CULTURAL CONTEXT

This is probably the last generation of pau at the camp as there are no current initiates and little indigenous interest, although there was years ago (Berglie 1983, 162). Berglie (1976, 86) wrote, "The *pau* were perhaps the most active religious functionaries in the settlement. Even more than the local lama, they come into contact with the intimate and personal problems of the villagers. Their séances were popular and spectacular events where people gathered and met.... I think it safe to say that the *pau* acted in the center of the religious life of the village."

Based on my experiences in the camp since 1996, such a situation seems difficult to imagine. The healing rituals I've attended over the years never had a large camp audience, only a few family members. Years ago, I had heard stories about some of Wangchuk's rituals being well attended, but this was before I had met him. As I recall, it was in 2000 that he became too ill to practice regularly albeit he attempted to accommodate anyone who came to his house for treatment (Sifers 2007, 41; Sifers and Peters 2001, 32).

In 2003, Rhichoe, as well as Nyima, had a small indigenous practice. They did some of the work Wangchuk was no longer able to do, and both periodically traveled to Kathmandu and the other camps as needed (Sifers 2005, 119). However, soon afterward, Rhichoe developed leg problems incapacitating him for even this irregular travel. I know that since 2005, his income has been almost entirely dependent on Western touring group patients and his meager wages at the camp carpet factory. He rarely sees clients. He has recently been named a Living Treasure of FSS, as has Pau Nyima, positions that will provide them with an annual stipend.

At the present time, Nyima has a small indigenous practice of perhaps five to six clients weekly, mostly Nepalese, also one or two Western trekkers monthly, plus European and American touring groups. In 2005, Nyima was invited to Vienna to do healings. Rhichoe is not as active physically, and is also a very private person, much less gregarious than Nyima. Further, Rhichoe's rituals are long events, lasting almost three hours, whereas Nyima's are an hour at most. Thus Nyima does more shamanism, as he is more available and requires less of a time commitment. They are both known to be highly effective healers.

Still, Nyima, like Rhichoe, and Wangchuk before them, relies on the fees and grants he earns from foreigners. If not for this income and acknowledgment, camp shamanism would have far less status than currently. In thirty-plus years, the community-central and once robust practice of camp shamanism is on the verge of disappearing.

The crisis of exile transplanted shamanism from its natural environment—the mountains, snow, and nomadic way of life—into a tropical climate and the sedentary life-way of a refugee population unable to return to the homeland and sacred places once alive with the stories that put shamanism in context and gave meaning to life. The pau often speak with great fondness of their former nomadic life and with great passion about their desire to return home. Indeed, exile was and continues to be traumatic in the lives of these men.

The present threat to shamanism was preceded by a much earlier one: Buddhism. As discussed, it converted the Bön deities and was, to a large measure, successful because it assimilated and textualized indigenous folk beliefs and shamanic practices. This was quite evident in the archival Lamaist text on the "soul calling" ritual in which traditional Bön beliefs regarding the soul as well as a sacrificial element have a prominent role, all of which are antithetical to Buddhist scripture. Similarly, the initiatory practice of ché, whose origins belong to prehistory and shamanism, became a Lamaist contemplative practice. On the other hand, shamanism has assimilated from Buddhism the tsa system, which is based on a Buddhist medicine and meditation system that explicitly recognizes the kyang ma, ro ma, and uma tsa, albeit their locations in the body are different than in shamanism (Dummer 1988, 12; Govinda 1960, 103). And it seems there is little difference between a Buddhist *chakra* (the Sanskrit term for "centers of subtle energy in the body") and the shaman's saug tsa, itself a center in which the tsa converge.[23] Further, the mediumistic trance of the pau is understood as a method of refuge, a Buddhist concept and practice, though to the pau it is a prelude to healing.

The pau at the refugee camp, as mentioned, distinguish between possession and refuge. In their role as spirit mediums, they do not become the deity, but an emanation. This gives the pau the powers not only of the refuge deity, but of the entire retinue of spirit helpers that are within the deity's emanations to utilize as needed, even to send on journeys. This seems to be unique, or unusual, for mediums, channels, or for possession-trance in general. However, it is the essential definitional feature and characteristic of shamanism. Thus a free soul is not necessary for shamanic journeying, as the pau can dispatch any member of the deity's retinue to do whatever is necessary and witness the entire process in the mirror (ling).

In the cultural-historical process that Bellezza (2005, 10) calls the "buddhacization of the indigenous pantheon and ritual practices," shamanism became devalued, marginalized, and subordinated to Buddhism, as reflected in the myth of Milarepa and Naro Bön Jung's contest mentioned earlier. With the loss of the nomadic culture that supported shamanism, and the religious life of the camp now centered around the monastery, the historical process of marginalization has accelerated.

Thus shamanism plays a decidedly smaller role in community life than it did in 1970–1971 when Berglie did his research. At that time, the monastery had only ten monks, and Tashi Palkhiel only four hundred residents (Berglie 1976, 87). Berglie (1992, 364–365) writes of the astonishing growth of the monastic compound in his revisit. Currently there are 120 monks and construction continues. There are very limited educational and job opportunities available as the Tibetans have only refugee status in Nepal, and the monastery offers the opportunity for a Buddhist education and community recognition. Buddhism is the solidifying community force and the authority on religious and moral issues. Although there is a strong hereditary element in shamanism, Buddhism is the choice of the children of the pau, who have spiritual beliefs.

Camp lama and pau have overlapping responsibilities; often they are called upon for the same reasons, to heal the sick or help overcome life obstacles. This is a major factor contributing to an ongoing assimilation process in which the pau are being replaced. It is not unusual to have a shamanic ritual and follow it with the same-purpose lama ritual. "Just to make sure," I was told by one camp resident. Pau Nyima became upset if it happened after one of his treatments. Nevertheless, when Nyima's brother failed to respond to his treatments, a lama was asked to do a healing ritual that dealt with the same troublesome spirits.

Traditionally, the pau have exclusive areas of expertise: the treatment of rabies, epilepsy, and a deadly bite from an insect (*sap sok*) found only in Tibet. This is not enough to sustain a vocation in the refugee camp. All other illnesses, whether they are caused by any of the various classes of deities or harmful né pa spirits or from fright, are treated by camp lama as well as pau. Lama and shamans are competitors. No matter that shamanism is rationalized as a "relative reality"; among most learned Buddhists, it is perceived as superstition. Thus the powerful practice of shamanism, traditionally an integral part of the pastoral community, transported from Tibet, was relevant at the camp for a few decades, but is now passing as the older generation who remember the old ways die, and the younger seeks fulfillment in less traditional vocations or in Buddhism.

REFERENCES

Baker, I. "Living Treasure Status Delights Tibetan Shaman." *Foundation for Shamanic Studies Newsletter* 4, no. 3 (1991): 6, 7.

Baumer, C. *Bön: Tibet's Ancient Religion.* Trumbull, CT: Weatherhill Inc., 2002.

Bellezza, J. V. *Spirit Mediums, Sacred Mountains and Related Bön Textual Traditions in Upper Tibet.* Boston: Brill, 2005.

Berglie, P. A. "Preliminary Remarks on Some Tibetan 'Spirit Mediums' in Nepal." *Kailash* IV, no. 1 (1976): 85–108.

———. "On the Question of Tibetan Shamanism." *Tibetan Studies: Papers Presented at the Seminar of Young Tibetologists,* edited by M. Braven and P. Kvaerne, 39–51. Zürich: Völkerkundemuseum der Universität Zürich, 1978.

———. "Spirit-Possession in Theory and Practice: Séances with Tibetan Spirit-Mediums in Nepal." *Religious Ecstasy,* edited by N. Holm, 151–166. Stockholm: Almqvist & Wiksell, 1982.

———. *The Gods Descend: Ritual Possession among Sherpas and Tibetans.* Stockholm: Akademisk Arhandling, 1983.

———. "Tibetan Spirit-Mediumship: Change and Continuity." *Tibetan Studies: Proceedings of the 5th Seminar of the International Association for Tibetan Studies,* Vol. 2, edited by S. Ihara and Z. Yamaguchi, 361–368. Tokyo: Narita, 1992.

Beyer, S. *The Cult of Tara.* Berkeley: University of California Press, 1973.

Das, S. C. *A Tibetan English Dictionary.* Berkeley, CA: Shambhala Booksellers, 1974.

Dummer, T. *Tibetan Medicine.* London: Routledge, 1988.

Dunham, C., and I. Baker. *Tibet: Reflections from the Wheel of Life.* New York: Abbeville Publishing Group, 1993.

Ekvall, R. G. *Fields on the Hoof.* New York: Holt, Rinehart and Winston, 1968.

Eliade, M. *Shamanism: Archaic Techniques of Ecstasy.* Princeton, NJ: Princeton University Press, 1964.

Eliade, M. *Yoga: Immortality and Freedom.* Princeton, NJ: Princeton University Press, 1969.

Ermakov, D. *Bo and Bön.* Kathmandu: Vajra Publications, 2008.

Evans-Wentz, W. Y., ed. "An Epitome of the Life and Teachings of Tibet's Great Guru Padma Sambhava." In *The Tibetan Book of the Great Liberation,* 103–192. London: Oxford University Press, 1954.

———. "The Path of the Mystic Sacrifice." In *Tibetan Yoga and Secret Doctrines,* 277–333. London: Oxford University Press, 1958.

Goldstein, M. *The New Tibetan-English Dictionary of Modern Tibetan.* Berkeley: University of California Press, 2001.

Govinda, A. *Foundations of Tibetan Mysticism.* New York: Samuel Weiser, 1960.

Grof, S. *Beyond the Brain.* Albany: State University of New York, 1985.

Harner, M. *The Way of the Shaman,* 2nd ed. San Francisco: Harper-Collins, 1990.

Hoffmann, H. *The Religions of Tibet.* London: George Allen & Unwin, 1961.

Jäschke, H. A. *A Tibetan-English Dictionary.* London: Routledge & Kegan Paul, 1972.

Karmay, S. G. *The Arrow and the Spindle.* Kathmandu: Mandala Book Point, 1998.

Katz, R. "Education for Transcendence: Lessons from the !Kung *Zhu/Twasi.*" *Journal of Transpersonal Psychology* 5, no. 1 (1973): 136–155.

Lessing, F. D. "Calling the Soul: A Lamaist Ritual." *Semantic Philology* XI (1951): 264–284.

Li An-Che. "Bon: The Magico-Religious Belief of the Tibetan Speaking Peoples." *Southwestern Journal of Anthropology* IV, no. 1 (1948): 31–41.

Nebesky-Wojkowitz, R. de. *Where the Gods Are Mountains.* New York: Reynal & Co., 1955.

———. *Oracles and Demons of Tibet.* Kathmandu: Pilgrims Book House, 1993.

Peters, L. G. "Trance, Initiation, and Psychotherapy in Tamang Shamanism." *American Ethnologist* 9, no. 1 (1982): 21–46.

———. "Mystical Experience in Tamang Shamanism." *ReVision* 13, no. 2 (1990): 71–85.

———. "Some Elements of the Tibetan Shamanism of Pau Wangchuk, Living Treasure of Shamanism." *Shamanism* 10, no. 2 (1997a): 21–23.

———. "The Tibetan Healing Rituals of Dorje Yüdronma." *Shaman's Drum* 45 (1997b): 36–47.

———. *Tamang Shamans.* New Delhi: Nirala, 1998.

———. *Trance, Initiation, and Psychotherapy in Nepalese Shamanism.* New Delhi: Nirala, 2004.

———. "The *Ghe-wa* (Tibetan Death Rite) for Pau Karma Wangchuk Namgyal." *Shamanism Annual: Journal of the Foundation for Shamanic Studies* 21 (2008): 2–7.

Rinpoche, Dagrab. *Buddhist Symbols in Tibetan Culture.* Boston: Wisdom Publications, 1995.

Samuel, G. *Civilized Shamans.* Washington, DC: Smithsonian Institution Press, 1993.

Sifers, S. "Fate of the Pau: Three Tibetan Shamans' Stories." *Shamanism* 18, nos. 1&2 (2005): 109–119.

———. "Letter from the Field." *Shamanism* 20, no. 1 (2007): 41.

———. *Fate of the Lhapa* (film). Watertown, MA: Documentary Educational Resources, 2008.

Sifers, S., and L. G. Peters. "Pau Wang Chuk: Status Report on FSS First Living Treasure." *Shamanism* 14, no. 1 (2001): 31–34.

Snellgrove, D., and H. Richardson. *A Cultural History of Tibet.* New York: Praeger, 1968.

Stein, R. *Tibetan Civilization.* Stanford, CA: Stanford University Press, 1972.

Tucci, G. *The Religions of Tibet.* Berkeley: University of California Press, 1988.

GLOSSARY OF FOREIGN TERMS

Phonetic	Tibetan Transliteration (Das 1974)	Meaning
atma		Sanskrit: soul
bar mee or *par mee*	*bar mi*	intermediary
Bön		indigenous shamanic tradition
Bön *ree*	Bön *ri*	Bön mountain
bum pa (or *ba*)		sacred offering bowl
chakra		Sanskrit: bodily centers of subtle energy
ché	*gcöd*	to "cut off"
ché pa	*gcöd pa*	a shaman who, in trance vision, sacrifices body
chos skyong		Tibetan oracles
dang	*mdangs*	glow of health
dharmapala		Sanskrit: converted Bön deity
dharu		shortened form of Sanskrit *dhamaru,* small drum
dip	*grib*	defilement
gufa		Nepali: cave initiation that includes *ché*
gyub dro	*skyabs hgro*	to take refuge
gyur wa	*hgyur ba* or *sgyur ba*	transformation, translation

Phonetic	Tibetan Transliteration (Das 1974)	Meaning
hé dzer	*höd gdser*	light or radiance
jib	*hjib*	shamanic extraction by sucking
jug pa	*hjug pa*	possessed
khadoma	*mkhah hgro ma*	"sky-going goddesses," Sanskrit: *dakhini*
khatak	*kha btags*	silk greeting scarf with eight signs of good fortune
kuk	*hgugs*	to call, activate, make shine, assemble, enrich
kyang ma tsa	*rkyang ma rtsa*	vein from fourth finger of right hand to heart
la	*bla*	soul
la kuk	*bla hgugs*	ritual to call the soul
la kyem pa	*bla hkhyams pa*	soul abandons body at death
la lug	*bla lug*	soul sheep and *spag* image
la né	*bla gnas*	place of the soul
la nyam	*bla nyams*	weakening of the soul
la ree	*bla ri*	soul mountain
la tsho	*bla mtsho*	soul lake
la yu	*bla gyu*	soul turquoise

Phonetic	Tibetan Transliteration (Das 1974)	Meaning
lama	*bla ma*	Buddhist priest
lang wa	*lang ba*	to rise
lha		heavenly deity or deity in general
lhamo		shaman or god woman (spirit medium)
lhapa		shaman or god man (spirit medium)
lha pab pa	*lha hbab pa*	descent of the deities
ling	*gling*	brass mirror, world
lu	*klu*	lower world and bodies of water serpent deities
luh	*glüd*	substitute offering in likeness of victim
mig pa	*dmig pa*	envision, visualize
nam shé	*nam çes*	consciousness
Né Jung	Gnas Cung	Tibetan State Oracle
né pa	*gnöd pa*	harmful spirits in general
ngak	*sngags*	reading and chanting from holy text
ngak pa	*sngags pa*	half-shaman, half-*lama*
nor bu		precious jewels of Buddhism

Phonetic	Tibetan Transliteration (Das 1974)	Meaning
nu shug	*nus shugs*	power, strength, energy
nyam pa	*nyams pa*	to decline
nyan	*gnyan*	middle world mountain deities
pab pa		descent of a deity's emanations
pahmo	*dpah mo*	shaman or female spirit medium
pau	*dpah bo*	shaman or male spirit medium
pret		Sanskrit: hungry ghost, graveyard ghost
rab né	*rab gnas*	consecrate
rig pa		reasoning, intelligence, understanding
ringa	*rigs lnga*	shaman's headdress
rinpoché	*rin po che*	educated and high-ranking priest
ro ma tsa	*ro ma rtsa*	vein from fourth finger of left hand to heart
saug	*srog*	breath soul, life force
saug tsa	*srog rtsa*	vein in center of chest, root of life, vein of life
see	*sri*	demons that bring death in a family

Phonetic	Tibetan Transliteration (Das 1974)	Meaning
sem	*sems*	mind, thinking
shakti		Sanskrit: power
shang	*gshang*	flat bell
shee dré	*çi dre*	ghost
spag	*spags*	barley flour dough
sten	*bstan*	one type of middle world deity
stupa		reliquary shrine
sung mo	*srung mo*	*dharmapala* or converted Bön deities
Tee Tsee	Ti Rtse (or Ti Si)	Mt. Kailash
tsa	*rtsa*	veins or channels in the body
tsampa	*rtsam pa*	barley flour
Tee Jung	Ti Cung	mountain given to Bön when lost Tee Tsee
tshé	*tshe*	life
tshé kuk	*tshe hgugs*	life calling
tshé wang	*tshe dbang*	long life empowerments
tulpa	*sprul pa* (or *ba*)	emanations of the deity
uma tsa	*dbu ma rtsa*	channel or vein from heart to head
wang	*dbang*	empowerment

Phonetic	Tibetan Transliteration (Das 1974)	Meaning
yee dzik	*yi dsigs*	demons with huge bellies that cause illness (*pret*)
yul lha		"country gods" or local protective deities
zhee dak	*gshi bdag*	deities or lords of mountains, rivers, bridges

·2·

SOUL *in* CONTEMPORARY TIBETAN SHAMANISM[24]

The purpose of this chapter is to continue the discussion of the boundaries of the soul in the belief system of the FSS Tibetan "Living Treasures" in the articles published in the *Shamanism Annual* each year since 2008. Tibetan culture is notable for the attention given to the after-death experience. Books have been written, mostly by lama describing the journey of the dead, the most famous being *The Tibetan Book of the Dead.* Little, however, has been written about the soul of the living person. This chapter focuses on the state of the soul in trance, health, and illness. These are the areas in which the Tibetan shaman has expertise.

In order to give proper attention to the nature of the soul in contemporary Tibetan shamanism, it is necessary to consider four factors:

1. The practice of the la kuk tshé kuk (life prolongation rite), the principal ritual for the rehabilitation of the soul.
2. The shaman's embodiment trance.
3. Buddhist influence on shamanic belief and practice.
4. Tibetan shamanism in exile and the effects of acculturation.

Pau (shaman, literally brave)[25] Nyima Dhondup, who is seventy years old, is the current FSS Tibetan Living Treasure (see Figure 2-1). He resides and practices shamanism at the Tashi Palkhiel (Auspiciousness Blossoming) refugee camp outside Pokhara, Nepal. Tashi Palkhiel has a population of about 1,400. It was established in the early 1960s for Tibetans who escaped the Chinese invasion and occupation of their homeland.

The work of Pau Nyima is significant, as he is the focus of attention in most studies of the life prolongation rite. Nyima is the subject of the portion of a highly acknowledged ethnographic report on the shamans at the refugee camp that focuses on the la kuk tshé kuk rite (Berglie 1976, 1983). He is featured in the part of a film on the shamanism in the camp depicting the la kuk tshé kuk ceremony (Sifers 2008), and there is a detailed description of Nyima's performance (Peters 2009).

The la kuk tshé kuk is only a very small fraction of Pau Nyima's extensive ritual repertoire. Extraction-type healings constitute the vast majority of his rituals. However, Nyima is a recognized authority on la kuk tshé kuk in his culture and among foreign students of shamanism. Nyima has traveled to Austria and Russia and performed the ritual there, as well as in Kathmandu on occasion. Nyima has done the la kuk tshé kuk ritual for ill members of visiting foreign groups, and it is done for camp residents and for his Nepali patients.[26] The latter appear to be the major part of his domestic clientele.

Apparently no researchers observed and wrote about the late Pau Wangchuk, the FSS first Living Treasure, performing this rite before his death in 2008. Another of the Living Treasures, Pau Pasang Rhichoe, passed in March 2012, but had not done it in perhaps forty years. It appears that the la kuk tshé kuk is Nyima's specialty. I have had the good fortune of having observed Pau Nyima perform the rite three times and have questioned him about these in detail. Thus Pau Nyima is the focus of this chapter.

SHAMANISM AND BUDDHISM

It is often stated that the major reason for the "Buddhization" of Tibet was Buddhism's ability to assimilate the indigenous Tibetan "folk religion" (or Bön) and its shamanic practices into its belief system.

Figure 2-1. Pau Nyima Dhondup. Photo by Amber McDonald, 2010.

Buddhism came to Tibet in the mid-eighth century CE and, since that time, it is also true that Tibetan shamanism has incorporated many Buddhist beliefs into its practice. When asked about the relationship of shamanism to Buddhism, Nyima says that, although Buddhism and shamanism are totally separate entities, they have many common beliefs because the ideas of both have been "mixed together." Thus Buddhism and shamanism share some features and have influenced each other's development, but Buddhist belief and practice are central to contemporary Tibetan culture.

Shamanism is not a religion. The pau are Buddhist. Their devotion to Buddhism is apparent in their altars, which are prominently displayed in their homes. These contain photos of H. H. the Dalai Lama and other venerated Buddhist lama, as well as statues and paintings of Buddhist deities. The pau turn prayer wheels or count *mala* beads while softly pronouncing Buddhist mantra[27] and prayer throughout the entire day, every day, stopping only when they need to free their right hands for a necessary task.

The sacred healing practice of the pau is not contrary to Buddhism. Nyima says that the work of the pau has the same purposes as that of the lama, albeit they are achieved in a different manner, and with distinct "nonordinary reality" forces (see Figures 2-2, and 2-3). The deities the pau specifically invoke in their rituals are not the high-ranking heavenly lha deities of the lama, but the old deities of the folk religion now converted to Buddhism. They are middle world, of lesser status, and, unlike the lha, not considered enlightened, but have taken a sacred vow to defend Buddhism and its institutions. The heavenly ranking of the deities is a mirror image of the social hierarchy of the shaman vis-à-vis the status-dominant lama: as above, so below. At the refugee camp, Buddhism and its monastery of 120 monks is the most powerful social and moral authority.

The folk belief in soul, too, has undergone changes during nearly 1,300 years of Buddhism. Even today, many of the old pre-Buddhist elements persist, albeit these, like the indigenous deities, have over time been woven into the fabric of the prevailing Buddhist belief system.

SOULS

Pau Nyima recognizes three souls: the *la,* the *tshe,* and the *nam shé.* As the name of the life prolongation rite (la kuk tshé kuk) indicates, the la and the tshe souls are the focus of the healing rite. It is also likely that they are indigenous concepts of the folk religion that predate Buddhism (Tucci 1988). The la is composed of the cosmic divine "energy," "force," "power," "strength," "vigor," or "ardor" inherent in a person. This inner force of supernal origin is called nu shug in Tibetan. Pau Nyima identifies nu shug as having similarities to the Nepali and Indian concept of shakti.[28] Nu shug animates the body and stimulates the mind. When a person's la is diminished in nu shug, he is disempowered and weakened in body and mind, and lacks passion and motivation. Additionally, his complexion changes; he loses his "shine" or "glow" and becomes pale. This is because the corporal manifestation of nu shug is light. When healthy, a person radiates like the sun and moon, as if infused with their cosmic light, and is in harmony with the universe, life has few obstacles, and one's luck is great. But, when he loses nu shug, he is in disharmony, his appearance is dull, luck has turned sour, and the person is susceptible to serious, life-threatening diseases of blood, bone, and organ. This unhealthy, weakened condition of the la is called la nyam and is a basic reason that la kuk tshé kuk is performed; that is, to restore nu shug, as, without a necessary quantity, the person's la will continue to deteriorate, la nyam will become more debilitating, and the person will get weaker, until he eventually dies. The total depletion of nu shug is tantamount to death.

Further, the la is a principal element of consciousness. It is the spirit inside that makes a person a conscious, thinking being. The la has the powers of perception, thinking, and intelligence. Without the necessary nu shug, these powers are weakened and mentation becomes confused and unreliable. Even the normal functioning of the five senses is impaired. Thus, when the la is diminished of nu shug, the mental activities that support consciousness are compromised. A severe loss might produce a coma. La kuk means "to return," "to restore," "to make shine," "to turn on," "to activate," and, according to Pau Nyima, "to raise" or "to increase" the diminished nu shug of the la.

The second soul is called the tshe. Tshe means life. It is the life soul.[29] The tshe is located in the body, in the area of the heart, at the place called the "root of life." It is also known as the "breath soul." It is the life-force spirit within us that opposes death and, after death, seeks rebirth. It is comparable to an immortal life instinct. The tshe can also become diminished in power (nu shug), which decreases the life instinct and thus needs to be restored to extend the present life span. The shamanic remedy for both la and tshe disempowerment is the la kuk tshé kuk rite.

As mentioned before, Tibetan shamanism has historically assimilated numerous Buddhist concepts. This includes the nam shé. Both la and nam shé are terms that Nyima regularly uses interchangeably and typically does not recognize a difference between them. Like the Buddhist he is, Nyima has merged the concept of the la with the nam shé. However, unlike lama, whose doctrine does not permit for a belief in a soul, Nyima considers the nam shé to be a soul. When asked how many souls a person possesses, Nyima says, "One, the nam shé." Never the la or tshe. It seems to me, from Nyima's description, that the nam shé is a kind of "oversoul," whereas the tshe and la have been subsumed within the scope of the nam shé, specifically its immortal life force (tshe) and consciousness (la) aspects, which, as mentioned above, are probably pre-Buddhist concepts. If so, and I believe it is, this is an example of what Nyima has called the "mixing together" of Buddhism and shamanism.

THE SHAMAN'S TRANCE

In the embodiment[30] trance of Nyima, he projects his nam shé from his body for a moment and "transfers" (*gyur wa*) it to his principal deity, who, in return, introjects some of its own light, power, and being into Nyima's mind and body (for details, see Peters 2009). This exchange is a very dangerous procedure and must be done instantaneously, if not simultaneously, or the shaman will immediately die without the presence of some of the deity's nu shug (light and power), life force, and consciousness to replace his own, and without the encircling protection of the deity's body of light that holds his exposed and vulnerable nam shé for the duration of the ritual and trance. Occasionally, Nyima figuratively says the deity embodies his nam shé while he embodies the deity's nam shé.

Sometimes Nyima speaks of his la being transferred, at other times the nam shé, but it is understood that all three souls are united and act as one. Like the la and tshe, the nam shé is bound to the body except during the shaman's embodiment trance. It is the only time the nam shé is out of the body of the shaman. Still, it cannot roam about or journey; the deity contains its activity, and it is restricted to one out-of-body location in the company of the invoked deity within one of the shaman's light-reflecting brass mirrors (ling) that is displayed on his altar, and there it remains inactive and out of the shaman's consciousness, which, as stated above, has been supplanted by elements of the consciousness of the embodying deity.

The deity that has been invoked and has taken control of the shaman's body speaks through him and performs the ritual for the benefit of the patient but, once this purpose is fulfilled, successfully or not, the deity will depart the shaman's body and return his nam shé. If the nam shé were to be otherwise occupied and not returned at the end of the ritual, when the deity's work is complete, the shaman's body would expire and the soul would not have a home to return to. It could then enter the death state (*bardo*) and there it might wander about until reincarnated. Or the soul might become lost and, as a ghost, continue to roam the earth (*la khyam*) (see Peters 2008, 2010).

The nam shé or la of the shaman does not journey in life, only in death. The instantaneous transference from the shaman's body to the protective custody of the deity does not qualify as more than an out-of-body experience. It is a prelude to embodiment, not to a journey. However, Nyima and the other pau are able to dispatch the members of their deity's numerous entourage of spirits to do healings at a distance, find lost objects, encounter ghosts, guide souls of the deceased, etc. And, all the while the deity's spirits are doing their work, the deity-embodied shaman has a vision (mig pa) of the process in one of the large brass mirrors on his altar.

Nyima does not believe that it is the same thing for his deity's spirits to be on a journey as it is for his soul (nam shé) to be on a journey. This is an important distinction in his mind. From his perspective, it is a life and death issue; as mentioned above, a soul journey is possible only after one has died. However, from the perspective of "core shamanism," as well as the psychology of visualization, Nyima's type of "spirit journey" does not seem to be substantially different from a "soul journey." Therefore, although Nyima, like other pau, is typically referred to as a "spirit medium" because he "channels" his principal deity, he also realizes a "shamanic state of consciousness" (Harner 1990) but does not soul journey per se.

In summary, Nyima does not believe the la and tshe to be separate from the nam shé and understands the nam shé to be bound to the body of the shaman in all circumstances, except during the embodiment trance. Otherwise, Nyima insists, without his nam shé (la and tshe), a shaman would quickly pass. Again, the shaman's trance is not subject to this fate only because his body has been filled by the presence of the deity and its powers until his nam shé is returned, and the power lent by the deity for the healing that had also served to sustain the shaman's body and life during the ritual, in the absence of his nam shé, is taken back by the deity, to end the trance and the ritual.

In the discussion of the process of the shaman's trance, we have seen that the shaman's out-of-body experience does not involve a soul journey. The boundaries of his soul are severely circumscribed. Momentarily, our attention will turn to the boundaries of the soul of patients and ordinary persons who are not shamans. If one studies the literature on the Tibetan shamanism practiced at the camp, it is curious that, while it is generally acknowledged that the shaman's trance is not a soul journey, the patient, on the other hand, is thought to lose soul after a traumatic fright. His nam shé then meanders about haphazardly from the body, lost for long periods, days if not months, and without the necessary deity embodiment that maintains the life of the shaman's physical body during the time his nam shé is out of his body, and without the immediate fatal consequences the shaman would suffer under similar conditions. How can it be that the boundaries of the soul of the shaman are highly restricted and, in the same cultural belief system, the soul boundaries of the ordinary person have no such limitations? More than curious, it is incongruent, inconsistent, and cross-culturally without precedent (see Peters and Price-Williams 1980; Peters 1989).

THE SHAMAN'S LANGUAGE

It was in the early 1970s that Berglie, a student of comparative religion, questioned Nyima about his la kuk tshé kuk. Berglie never witnessed the rite in the year he lived in the camp. Pau Wangchuk and Rhichoe did not perform it, but Nyima did and Berglie received a description of it from Nyima. And, from what seems to be a very incomplete description, Berglie (1976, 1983) developed the idea of "soul loss" in Tibetan shamanism. Ethnographers writing about Tibetan shamanism frequently quote Berglie's study and assume that the data they are working with reflects the same notion. However, there are only a few reports, and these are anecdotal and incomplete, of other shamans besides Nyima performing the rite. Thus, Nyima's practice of la kuk tshé kuk, which is recorded in the FSS journal (Peters 2009) and film (Sifers 2008), are the most detailed descriptions available (see Figure 2-4).

One problem is that Nyima has apparently been inconsistent over the years. From 1996 to 2008, he told me about soul loss, just as he had told Berglie many years earlier. Nearly a decade ago, he told the same thing to another investigator, adding details of fragmented soul parts leaving the body (Sifers 2005). In 2008, Nyima told me the opposite, that the soul (la or nam shé) was bound to the body. I knew at the time that this new information was contrary to the findings of competent researchers. Thus I cross-checked with Pau Rhichoe, and questioned both Nyima and Rhichoe many times in 2008 and 2009, in order to verify the new data. I thought I had been thorough before *Shamanism* published my 2009 article. However, recently, Sifers (2011) raised doubts that have required a follow-up and a review of the ethnographic discovery process specifically on the issue of soul loss.

In 2008, Nyima flatly told me that, if the la leaves the body, a person will quickly die. This confused me at the time, as he had previously identified la kuk tshé kuk as a ritual means of calling back a lost la soul. I wrote, in 2009, "I protested to Pau Nyima that, in order to be called back, as in the la kuk tshé kuk ceremony, the la would first need to leave the body ... Nyima got up, threw his hands up, slapped them against his sides, obviously frustrated, and complained that I didn't understand the la. He left the house (for ten minutes) ... When he returned, I asked him what term he used for 'soul loss' ... After [Nyima's lengthy animated discussion with Migmar, my translator and] a long pause [gathering her thoughts], Migmar said, 'There is no such idea. [Nyima says] the pau do la kuk tshé kuk because the patient's la has been damaged and is deteriorating.'" In other words, la nyam.

For me, this was a dramatic learning experience that changed my perspective of the la and of the la kuk tshé kuk rite. It did for Migmar as well, who, up to this time, had mistranslated la nyam as a loss of soul instead of a loss of soul power (nu shug) or shakti; that is, a disempowerment that weakens the la and causes the deterioration of body and mind described above. I know, from my own experience, that Migmar received quite a bit of reinforcement for this misinterpretation. It was in sync with the principles of core shamanism, my expectations, and ostensibly what Nyima had told other researchers. Migmar knew that her translation did not match her understanding, nor the dictionary definition. She believed, from years of translating for him, that the context in which Nyima used la nyam dictated a "little" different interpretation. In retrospect, she was dismayed at her confusion. Later, we will discuss how this happened. Regardless, Migmar was not aware of the core principles that define shamanism. She is not a Tibetan shaman, nor was she aware of Tibetan shamanic terminology, nor was I until Migmar and I began to study it together in 2008.

After this experience with Nyima, I realized that I had been completely dependent on lay translators since beginning fieldwork at the camp, translators who knew little about Tibetan shamanism and, that if I was going to find my way out of confusion, I needed to study the shamanic nomenclature or I would be limited by the knowledge of the uninitiated.

Thus another phase of fieldwork began in 2008, one in which the focus was on the study of the shaman's technical language. Since that time, Migmar and I spent many days researching texts and scouring dictionaries for the meanings of terms Nyima used to describe his shamanic practice. Migmar was a great asset, and I had studied "classical" Tibetan for three years as an anthropology graduate student some years ago, which also proved invaluable. For the study of the soul, I was particularly interested in those terms preceded by la, which changes the understanding of a word to include the idea of the soul. For example, *nyam* means "to be weakened or damaged," la nyam "the weakened or damaged la."

Migmar and I started to discuss the terms and what we learned about them from various sources with Nyima and, when he began to extrapolate on the meaning of the terms, significant new data arose that had not been mentioned previously. Further, I was impressed with the knowledge Nyima possesses about his profession, more than before, as the discussion of the terms seemed to unearth a previously buried wisdom.

Sifers (2011) has stated that there is no such category of illness as the disempowerment of the soul, i.e., la nyam. In part, she believes that I came to this conclusion due to Migmar's (and therefore my) lack of skill at translation and that the concepts of soul loss and soul retrieval were substantiated by the U.S.-based, off-site lay translator she employed for her film. Sifers does not mention any Tibetan terms. She only gives an English narrative, making it impossible to check for linguistic accuracy and thereby validate her claims. In other words, Sifers's critique is linguistic, dependent on a lay translator's understanding of technical terminology and subtleties of Tibetan shamanism.

Nonetheless, I decided it was necessary to requestion Nyima on his la kuk tshé kuk, on his definitions of la, la nyam, and another term, la khyam, which means "wandering about of the la," i.e., about soul loss, in order to make sure once again that Nyima, Migmar, and I had achieved an accurate mutual understanding of key Tibetan terms and concepts.

Thus, in 2012, I made a sound recording of an interview with Nyima and had it translated by Migmar and two other reliable sources. In the following interview, I was careful to include the Tibetan term in the question in an effort to verify the existence of the term, its meaning, and relevance to Nyima's practice of la kuk tshé kuk.

LP (author): What is the meaning of la nyam?

Translation by Migmar Choezam (field assistant/translator and former camp English teacher): The person becomes weak. He loses nu shug. There is no glow or shine to his look. All the five senses are weakened. Thinking is not right.

Translation by Urgyen Dawa (teacher of "classical" Tibetan language and culture): A person becomes weak and loses power. The glow is weak and pale, and every sense organ is weakened. Thinking is not right.

LP: Is la nyam the reason why pau do the la kuk tshé kuk?

Migmar translation: Yes, and by saying prayers and *sutra,* strength will slowly return.

Dawa translation: Yes, and by reciting Buddhist sutra, the strength will slowly come back.

LP: If the la leaves the body—la khyam—will the person remain alive?

Migmar translation: If the la goes out, then the person dies.

Dawa translation: When a person dies, the la leaves the body. Otherwise, no.

LP: Is there a part la? Can a piece of the la break off and leave the body?

Migmar translation: There are no parts, no half parts breaking off, going out, and coming back.

Dawa translation: There is no half la. No parts coming and going.

LP: Is the purpose of la kuk tshé kuk to strengthen the la and the tshe?

Migmar translation: Yes, to become more healthy and to glow.

Dawa translation: Yes, to become stronger and to glow.

The substantial accuracy of the above translations was verified by Khedup Rinpoche, a PhD, Buddhist scholar, and periodically a teacher at the camp monastery.

The recitation of sutra[31] (teachings of the Buddha) is a supplementary means of strengthening the la, and refers to Nyima's advice to the patient after the ritual has ended, to read the sutra and "take refuge" in the Buddha. That is, to meditate and ask for guidance from the Buddha. Furthermore, Nyima sometimes recommends that the patient ask lama to do a daylong ritual sutra reading in order to quicken full recovery from la nyam. In other words, Nyima's experience is that remission of symptoms is not immediate and that devotion to Buddhism and the aid of lama will be beneficial.

The principal part of the la kuk tshé kuk that is relevant for this chapter and to the above translation is that Nyima, while embodied by deity, gives three types of stone to the patient near the end of the ritual, which the patient wears as an amulet thereafter. The most important of these stones is a single turquoise (see Peters 2009). Turquoises are valued for their brilliance and symbolism, and nearly everyone wears one. If they blanch, as those of poor quality might do, they are traditionally discarded, and a new, bright one found. They are symbols of health as well as talismans that provide protection from nefarious spirits, but when they become dull, they lose their protective powers against disease and ill luck.

The turquoise is called la yu, or "soul turquoise," but Nyima says that it is a mistake to see the soul turquoise given to the patient in the rite as indicating a soul retrieval. The turquoise is not the repository of the la. However, the turquoise possesses an abundance of cosmic divine power and light (nu shug). Its brilliance is the same as that of the sun and moon, and, at the same time, it is the "glow" or "shine" of the healthy person in harmony with the universe. In other words, there is a "sympathetic identity" that connects the healthy, radiant soul to the emanations of the heavenly bodies and to the glow of the turquoise. The principle of sympathy states "like produces like." Thus, by giving a brilliant turquoise to the patient, Nyima restores the luminous glow of health upon the patient. The glow is a physical sign that the nam shé (la and tshe) have been activated, invigorated, and infused with cosmic divine light and power, and thereby "made to shine" (la kuk tshé kuk). The life prolongation rite is a light and power restoration to a dull, disempowered nam shé (la and tshe). The la kuk tshé kuk is a soul healing rite and not a soul retrieval. The latter would require an errant soul.

The ethnographic and linguistic data presented above seems to be ample proof that the soul (nam shé, la, tshe), due to its restrictive boundaries, does not soul journey as such, and soul retrieval and soul loss are not part of the Tibetan belief system. Still, it is difficult to comprehend from the above how it could be that, over many years, three translators I know of who worked with Nyima had made the same error. To see into this mystery, we need to widen our lens in order to look beyond the refugee camp, which does not exist in a cultural vacuum but is a part of the greater Nepali society.

SHAMANISM AND ACCULTURATION

Before I could interview Nyima for a second time in 2012 (see Figure 2-5), he invited me to his house for another la kuk tshé kuk rite. This would be the third time I witnessed Nyima doing the ritual. The first time was for ill members of one of my educational groups, the second was for a Nepali man, as was the third. All three had the same observable elements. This third healing was for a man who was too weak to travel. His nephew represented him in absentia. The patient was supposed to attend; however, the young man had traveled far and Nyima did not want to disappoint him nor the patient, so he consented to do a "long-distance" la kuk tshé kuk.

During the rite, the deity embodying Nyima spoke through him in Tibetan. The shaman's assistant and intermediary (bar mee) is the designated person present who is allowed to speak to the deity, and the deity only speaks directly to the bar mee. Everyone else, including the patient, speaks to the deity only indirectly through the bar mee. For Nepali patients, Karma, Nyima's brother and interpreter, speaks to the client in Nepali; that is to say, he translates for the deity into

Figure 2-5. Larry Peters interviewing Pau Nyima with Tashi (Nyima's wife) and translator Migmar Choezam (far right). Photo by Amber McDonald, 2010.

Nepali, because these patients do not speak Tibetan. Thus, each time the deity spoke, Karma translated it into Nepali and, when the client wished to speak to the deity, Karma translated the Nepali into Tibetan, even though Nyima speaks Nepali well. The only term that the deity spoke that Karma did not need to translate was the Nepali term for a soul: *saato.* I also understood some of the Nepali and recognized that Karma was telling the young man that his sick uncle had "lost soul!" (*saato gayo* in Nepali).

This was not a surprise, as Nyima had explained this in 2010, the second time I observed the la kuk tshé kuk (see Figure 2-6). At that time, Nyima said that the deity knows the thinking of the patient and so the deity speaks to them according to the way they understand; that Nepali do not believe in the la, so the deity tells them about the saato and not about the la, nor the nam shé. However, the Nepali saato, unlike the Tibetan la, can wander from the body. It can get lost and captured, and many Nepali shamans do soul retrievals (see Peters 1998).

In other words, Nepali do not believe in soul disempowerment as a category of illness, like the Tibetans. There is no equivalent to la nyam, but they do believe in soul loss. Nyima has found his la kuk tshé kuk to have more power and, I believe, to make himself more acceptable to the larger Nepali population that does not reside in the camp, if he framed his rituals to be compatible to these patients' worldview. It is possible that Nyima learned about and became sensitive to belief in soul loss from his Nepali patients, and that their expectations and assumptions compelled him to align his explanations.

Be that as it may, saato has no relation to the la or to the tshe or nam shé, which are Tibetan concepts. The la does not wander and cannot fragment and lose parts of itself. When I had sound-recorded Nyima earlier, I asked him specifically about the la leaving the body, and he said "no." This reply was because I had been specific in asking him about the la, la nyam, and la khyam; that is, in Tibetan shamanic terms, leaving no doubt about what I desired to learn. And, in our time together since 2008, I have found that Nyima has been consistent as long as I was specific in my questioning. Still, it is evident from Nyima's own words that he has two distinct scenarios for his la kuk tshé kuk, each belonging to a different cultural belief system, either of which he is able to draw upon depending on context, one that he believes to be the true representative of his tradition and the other more efficacious with certain patients.

Indeed, if we are to believe what Nyima says, he has accommodated his system to meet the demands of the present situation of exile and thereby maintain a practice in the dominant Nepali culture. It is a strategy with survival value. As mentioned above, it is this part of his practice that is most active. It seems obvious to me that this is a shamanic belief system in transition that has required innovation in order to survive in a foreign culture.

At the camp, shamanism is no longer the viable community force it was forty years ago (Berglie 1976). There are no initiates, little interest, minimal work, and no social status ascribed to the shamans. In fact, the lama see shamanism as superstition and less than real. Some camp residents believe it is contrary to Buddhism and are fearful of it. Indeed, shamanism will quite probably cease to exist at the camp when Nyima passes.

Nyima's adaptive survival strategy has created much confusion for researchers and translators. This is because Nyima's two ritual motifs logically contradict one another; they are polar opposites. In one scenario, the la is "bound" to the body; in the other, the saato is "free" to roam. This disparity does not mean that Nyima misleads some researchers purposely while telling the truth to others, as Sifers (2011) contends. Nyima does not hide ritual information and didn't keep from sight the rituals that contradicted what he had previously told me to be true. Rather, he explained his motives once I specifically communicated what I desired to learn. Prior to 2008, I had not been explicit. I asked him about his practice and what he does during the ritual, but I hadn't contemplated that his explanations about what he was doing could be different for different populations. My research purpose was to know what he believes as a Tibetan shaman and not what he chooses to tell his Nepali patients, although that too is important, but for other reasons.

Only after learning the proper Tibetan terms for the souls and related concepts, and educating myself in partnership with Migmar by researching their meanings together, was it possible to ask very specific questions and thereby penetrate the Tibetan belief system. The terms grounded Nyima in the traditional system and provided the background to our discussion of how and why he frames the rite differently to suit his Nepali patients.

CONCLUSIONS

Language reflects what people think and it provides an empirical base that can be validated by a researcher with the ambition to do so, but it does not necessarily reveal what people will do in a challenging situation. The shaman's oral lexicon is key to comprehending the native belief system, but it cannot explain what is done in order to survive in the midst of massive social change; i.e., a violent exile from Tibet demanding a transition from the pastoral nomadism of a mountainous cold environment to a sedentary refugee camp lifestyle in a tropical valley, and the contemporary market economy of Nepal.

The differences in FSS research reports on the la kuk tshé kuk reflect the differences between the traditional shamanic belief system that has been influenced for more than a millennium by Buddhism and an adjusted current practice that accommodates the traditional beliefs to meet the demands of exile in Nepal. The similarities in research findings are in the area of the shaman's trance. In fact, there has been a reasonable consistency over many years, from Berglie's (1976) pioneering work to the first discussion in an FSS *Newsletter* (Baker 1991) to the present. This, I believe, is because the personal existential nature of the embodiment experience, especially the relationship to deity, is less susceptible to social pressure to conform than are interactive rituals.

If we juxtapose the two—the shaman's embodiment trance with its circumscribed boundaries of the soul, with the belief in soul loss—they are incongruous, because the sources of the two are from distinct cultural and shamanic belief systems analogous to the two contradictory themes Nyima has for the la kuk tshé kuk. Nyima's understanding of embodiment trance, his methods of induction, invocation of deity, the "transfer," the brass mirror, and the soul boundaries therein have remained true to Tibetan culture, whereas the frame that Nyima uses with most of his clientele, and evidently with most researchers, derives from the larger Nepali community in which the refugee camp is embedded, with its distinct cultural and shamanic belief systems, most of which include the belief in soul loss. Nyima is well aware that he is mixing two traditions, but when I attempted to point out to him that the two were logically inconsistent, his response resonated as true, yet I am unsure if he was commenting on my statement, giving a teaching, or both. He said, "Healing is all in the thinking; everything is in the thinking (*sempa*)."

This chapter has explored Pau Nyima's understanding of the la kuk tshé kuk and how it is framed in diverse cultural settings. It does not claim that Nyima's Tibetan shamanic belief system is pristine and free from Buddhist influence. Nor does it propose that his system is the same for all Tibetan shamans. This chapter presents only a case study of Pau Nyima's Tibetan shamanism, specifically his la kuk tshé kuk. His beliefs about the soul boundaries, however, might have wider application, as they are similar to a Tibetan shamanic practice in another location (see Peters 1997) and to that of the late Pau Rhichoe from the camp (see Peters 2009). That conclusion awaits further research. Limited though this chapter is, it is significant because Nyima is the source of most ethnographic studies on the la kuk tshé kuk. It is his ritual, with its inconsistent languaging in different cultures, that has received the most detailed descriptions.

REFERENCES

Baker, J. "Living Treasure Status Delights Tibetan Shaman." *Foundation for Shamanic Studies Newsletter* 4, no. 3 (1991): 6, 7.

Berglie, P. A. "Preliminary Remarks on Some Tibetan 'Spirit Mediums' in Nepal." *Kailash* (1976): 85–108.

———. *The Gods Descend, Ritual Possession among Sherpas and Tibetans.* Stockholm: Akademisk Arhandling, 1983.

Harner, M. *The Way of the Shaman.* San Francisco: HarperCollins, 1990 (originally published 1980).

Peters, L. G. "Shamanism: Phenomenology of a Spiritual Discipline." *Journal of Transpersonal Psychology* 21, no. 2 (1989): 115–137.

———. "The Tibetan Healing Rituals of Dorje Yüdronma." *Shaman's Drum* 45 (1997): 36–47.

———. *Tamang Shamans.* New Delhi: Nirala Publications, 1998.

———. "The *Ghe-wa* (Tibetan Death Rite) for Pau Karma Wangchuk Namgyal." *Shamanism Annual* 21 (2008): 2–7.

———. "Tradition, Practice, and Trance of the Foundation's Tibetan Living Treasures." *Shamanism Annual* 22 (2009): 2–20.

———. "Shaman as Psychopomp: Field Report on the Foundation's Living Treasures." *Shamanism Annual* 23 (2010): 25–29.

Peters, L., and D. Price-Williams. "Towards an Experiential Analysis of Shamanism." *American Ethnologist* 7, no. 3 (1980): 397–418.

Sifers, S. "Fate of the Pau: Three Tibetan Shamans' Stories." *Shamanism* 18, nos. 1&2 (2005): 109–119 (originally published 2003).

———. *Fate of the Lhapa* (film). Watertown, MA: Documentary Educational Resources, 2008.

———. "Soul Loss or Diminishment? A Re-examination of the Tibetan Living Treasures' *Lha Kuck* Ceremony." *Shamanism Annual* 24 (2011): 24–29.

Tucci, G. *The Religions of Tibet.* Translated by G. Samuel. Berkeley: University of California Press, 1988 (originally published 1970).

· 3 ·

SHAMAN *as* PSYCHOPOMP

This chapter is the result of ethnographic research conducted in March/April and August 2010 with Pau Nyima and Pau Rhichoe, in which I witnessed their healing work and had lengthy interviews with them afterward about the beliefs that explain their rituals, as well as about the contents of their trance experience. Its focus is the destiny of the soul, its vicissitudes after death, and the shaman's role as "guide of souls" or psychopomp.

GHOSTS

When I arrived for fieldwork in March 2010, I was disappointed to learn that I had just missed the *jin srik*[32] (a type of fire ceremony) attended by many residing in the Tibetan refugee camp of Tashi Palkhiel located near Pokhara, Nepal. I had heard previously about the ceremony in general terms and had spoken to the shamans (pau), a high-ranking lama (rinpoché), and others about it briefly.

Because it was now fresh in everyone's mind, I gave further time to its study. I learned that it is rarely performed and only when there are "numerous deaths" in the community. It is a three-day ceremony in which the *shed,* a type of spirit or soul of those deceased, are unable or unwilling to leave the bardo, or intermediate state after death and before rebirth, and are thus responsible for a high mortality rate in the community.[33] The ceremony is led by a rinpoché or, as in the camp ceremony, by a "Tantric Master" imported from a Buddhist monastery near Kathmandu, who was able to summon the shed of those who had died in the camp, guide them to follow the light, and send them from the bardo to a rebirth.

Although the elder shamans were not invited to play a role in the three-day refugee camp jin srik, traditionally shamans have the role in the ceremony of visioning (mig pa) where in the community the shed are to be found. At that point, the shamans or young men and monks (as in the recent ceremony) go to these places. They carry a sack (a sheep's belly) of a "soul sheep" (la lug) filled with the names of persons who have died in the previous five or six years. With the sack in hand, they gather up the shed (which expands the sack when the shed are caught) and bring them to the officiating lama, who will guide the shed to the lights of rebirth.

It is a fire ceremony because the names of the deceased, which are written on separate pieces of paper, are then poured out of the sack onto a metal plate. Papers that land written-side down will be burned. Those papers that land written-side up are returned to the sack, and the shamans again journey to discover the location of these shed. Thereafter, the process is repeated until all the written names are facedown and consumed in fire, at which time the shed guided by the lama are thought to have left the bardo and taken new births. Thus they will no longer be spirits that cause illness and death (né pa).

The la or "breath soul" is attached to the body in life. Its absence brings immediate death, and it ceases to exist when the person dies. Nam shé refers to the consciousness of the soul, and it is immortal. The shed is what the soul (or nam shé) can become at death; that is to say, if the forty-nine-day funeral ceremony (*ghe-wa*)[34] performed by lama has not been successful in unbinding the soul from the bardo—specifically if there is evidence to the contrary indicated by family members becoming ill after the recent death of a relative.

If so, the shaman might perform another type of fire ceremony, the *shed phud,* in which the shed will be "thrown"; that is, guided to the light by the shaman's spirits and hence out of the bardo. The shed phud is a healing ceremony for the living and at the same time a death ritual to psychopomp the soul to a new human birth. Pau Nyima says it is a healing for the shed as well, because it will lose its "attachments" to its former life and be reborn.[35]

The shed is not an evil spirit. It does not have evil intent. Rather, it is lost and roams close to those with whom it is familiar. However, the shed can cause illness and even death just by frequenting family. Most likely, it is attached to its recent past life and does not realize the harm it is causing.

A shed is formed by attachments. Therefore, a dead person might have numerous shed (soul parts), one for each attachment, possibly to a material object, but also to people and places. Pau Nyima describes a case he had in which a shed possessing a person (jug pa) caused much distress and anxiety to everyone in the household because a family member took for herself a favorite object of the deceased. This angered the shed, who attempted to repossess the object by embodying its new owner.

Nyima says that a shed with just one attachment is the most difficult to send from the bardo, because the attachment is very strong; the more attachments, the weaker the attachment to each respective object, and thus the easier it is to disengage the shed from its previous life.

It is the jin srik or community fire ceremony that is the last line of ritual defense to send away the dangerous and numerous shed—that is, when the number of deaths exceeds the concerns of any particular family and becomes a community problem. Consequently, it is a community ritual.

During their forty-nine-day funeral rite (ghe-wa), the lama try first to release the soul from the bardo. Then the shamans try to send the soul when it begins to be a family problem (shed phud). Then, finally, if these fail, and the result is that many people die, the lama and shamans traditionally work together toward the same end in the jin srik community ritual.

Shortly after death, the body is disposed of, cremated these days, but traditionally also butchered and offered to the holy thang kar birds of the high Himalayan ranges. If the body is not disposed of quickly, the soul could become a *ro lang* instead of becoming a shed; that is, the soul reoccupies and "raises up" (*lang*) its corpse. The ro lang is literally a stiff. It cannot bend, which is why Tibetans build their houses with low doorways. A ro lang is strong and dangerous. A person who is touched by a ro lang will become crazy.

Much stronger than a shed is the dre. Unlike the shed, the dre is a ghost with evil intent. There are numerous types of dre (fire dre, cemetery dre, etc.). A dre is a shed that has not left the bardo and has been roaming for a long and indeterminate time. A dre might enslave a shed and use it for its harmful designs, or assign the shed impossible tasks in order to cause it to become mad, like making ice in the summer heat.

However, the mental state of a person at the time of death is very important. If one dies with revenge in mind, for example, his nam shé (soul/consciousness) might immediately become a dre or a *dud mo* (spirit sorcerer) or even a sten (a type of demon; see next section). It is for this reason that much is done to keep a dying person in mental equanimity so that hateful or angry thoughts do not arise that could thereby keep the person's soul (nam shé) from leaving the bardo.

The above list of ghosts is not comprehensive. There are types and subtypes too numerous to mention. However, even with this limited information, a couple of general statements are possible: First, the bardo is not a realm or condition totally separate from the ordinary reality of the "substantial" world. The spirits of the dead, albeit insubstantial, have a direct effect on the living. And, while they are in the bardo, they simultaneously wander in a territory indistinguishable from middle world human existence. The trouble these ghosts cause is the basis for much shamanic work.

Further, the Lamaist funeral rituals (e.g., ghe-wa), the traditionally cooperative lama-shaman rite (e.g., jin srik), and the healing rituals of the shamans (e.g., the shed phud), while different in structure and content from each other, have similar aims, i.e., to aid the soul of the deceased (nam shé, shed, ro lang, or dre) to exit the bardo by finding a rebirth.

I mentioned to Nyima that, while the lama rituals of death and the healing rituals of the shamans look very different, the lama's being "peaceful" and those of the pau "wild," and ostensibly done for different situations and conditions, they both have a similar goal. His wife, Tashi, who is very knowledgeable of her husband's practice and whose father was also a shaman, answered for the hard-of-hearing Nyima, saying, "There are many different elements in shamanism and Buddhist practice (*gom*), but they are mixed together in the same bowl." That is to say, they are part of the same culture and thus their practices are based on a common worldview that includes beliefs about the fate of the soul.

BUDDHAS, DEMONS, AND DEMON DEITIES

In this section, the healing practices of Pau Rhichoe will be discussed, specifically the "dismemberment" and "rememberment" part of his healing rituals, and how they also have psychopompic elements. The dismemberment, sometimes called "skeletonization," is an essential feature of shamanism cross-culturally (Eliade 1964). Typically, it is the crucial and most critical part of the shaman's initiation.

With Rhichoe, however, it is part of many, if not all, of his healing rituals. He says, "I sacrifice my body to the né pa (general category of harmful spirits), my blood, bones, and flesh, so they will not consume those of the patient." Many of the né pa are the misfortune-creating ghosts discussed above. The dismemberment process is accompanied by a fast, loud, and rhythmic percussion of a small drum (dharu) in the right hand and a flat bell (shang) in the left (see Figure 3-1).

The deities and demons of all classes and ranks, as well as the ghosts, are first invoked. They come and take their places according to status within the altar mirrors (ling). Rhichoe uses two mirrors. The mirrors have three levels that correspond to the three levels of the cosmos—upper, middle, and lower worlds. When in trance (refuge), the shaman calls all these spirits to be present in the mirrors. When the spirits come, they arrive from the four directions and from above and below.

The term ling used for the mirrors primarily means "world." After the shaman has taken refuge, the mirrors "open" to a normally unseen world that has three doors: inner, outer, and middle. These again correspond to the three levels of the cosmos. The heavenly, upper world deities (*lha*) arrive through the open inner door. They come and are seated in the front of Rhichoe's uppermost altar mirror, which has now become a large tent or hall. The lha are all Buddhist deities, Buddhas and Bodhisattvas, and the ones that Rhichoe honors are pictured on his altar.

The srung mo[36] (demon deities) enter through the middle door and take their place behind the lha in the upper mirror. Srung mo are all middle world. They were once fierce Bön (indigenous religion of Tibet) deities of certain localities, like the sten, who are mostly mountain deities. The srung mo are all demons; the sten is one type of demon. What distinguishes the srung mo is that they were converted to Buddhism and made into deity defenders of Buddhism and its institutions. Srung mo are those converted by the Buddhist saint Padma Sambhava (a.k.a. Guru Rinpoche), who gave them a binding oath, thereby making them middle world Buddhist deity protectors. A srung mo can be the principal deity in which a shaman takes refuge (*kap*), i.e., absorbs their light through subtle channels or veins (*tsa*).[37]

Refuge is the prerequisite for nearly all shamanic work. The shamans take refuge only in the higher-ranking deities, i.e., lha or srung mo, but never in the sten or other types of unconverted demons, nor in the ghosts, all of whom are né pa, or spirits that may cause misfortune.

The lu (serpent deities) arrive through the outer door, and take their place in the lower mirror. They are the deities of the lower world but, when they appear on earth, they are associated with water:

■ **Figure 0-1.** Great Stupa. *Photo by Larry Peters.*

■ **Figure 1-1.** Altar of Pau Rhichoe. *Photo by Larry Peters.*

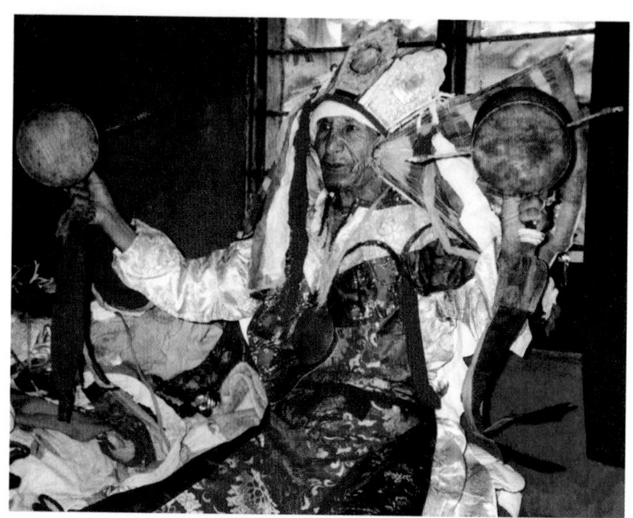

■ **Figure 1-2.** The late Pau Karma Wanchuk. *Photo by Larry Peters.*

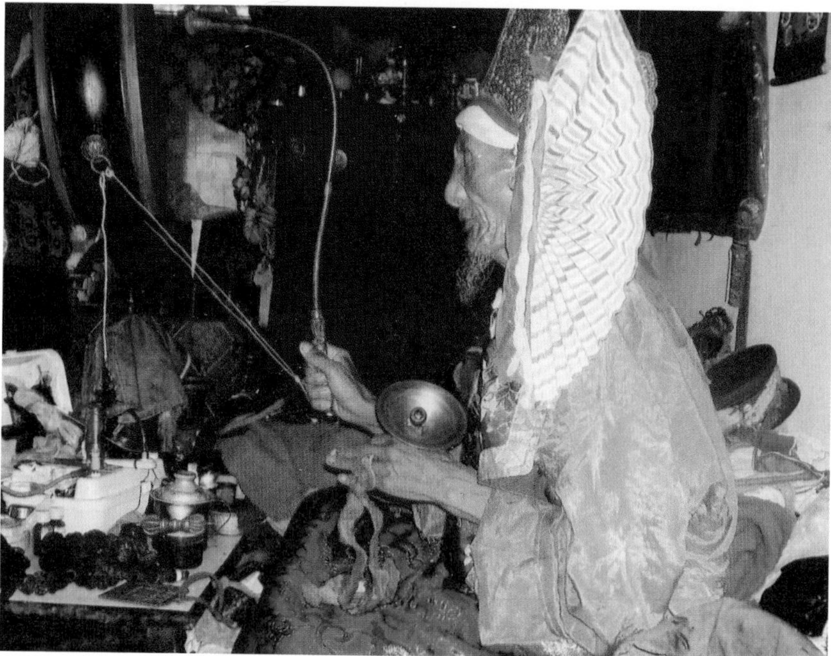

■ **Figure 1-3.** Pau Wangchuk playing the big nga chen (also known as the lama drum) with a large curved stick with string attached to the bottom of the stick and to the drum. As he prepared to hit the drum, the drum is pulled toward the stick. It is said that from the first sound of this drum the Iha (gods) descend from heaven, slowly like falling snow. At the second sound of the drum, the sten of the middle world will come like a hailstorm. At the third sound, the lower world leu will come like whirling snowflakes. *Photo and text by Larry Peters.*

■ **Figure 1-4.** An amulet to be worn after "soul calling." The shite shell (symbolizing bone) is a gift of the lower world serpent deities (lu); the coral (symbol of blood) is a gift of the mountain and red rock middle world sten; and the turquoise (symbol of the glow of health) is a gift from the heavenly gods (lha). *Photo by Sacha Guzy.*

■ **Figure 1-5.** Pau Wangchuk dance. The headdress wings (ringa) are like the rainbow on which the ascetic saint Milarepa ascended to the top of Mt. Kailash. *Photo by Larry Peters.*

■ **Figure 1-6.** The deity Thang Lha rides a white horse and carries a victory banner and the precious jewels of Buddhism (nor bu), which bring healing and equanimity of mind. *Photo by Larry Peters.*

■ **Figure 2-2.** Pau Nyima. *Photo by Amber McDonald, 2010.*

■ **Figure 2-3.** Pau Nyima with a patient. *Photo by Amber McDonald, 2010.*

■ **Figure 2-4.** The white scarf (or khata) is being held by Karma, Nyima's brother and "intermediary." When the deities arrive and embody Nyima, Karma puts the scarf between the lobes of Nyima's crown as a way to greet and honor them. Notice that there are numerous others from past rituals already in the crown. *Photo by Amber McDonald, 2010.*

■ **Figure 2-6.** Foundation for Shamanic Studies Living Treasure of Shamanism, Tibetan shaman Pau Nyama Dhondup. *Photo by Amber McDonald, 2010.*

■ **Figure 3-1.** The fully costumed Pau Rhichoe has "taken refuge" while sounding the flat bell (shang) and hand drum (dharu). *Photo by Amber McDonald.*

■ **Figure 6-1.** Wangchuk, performing a healing ritual, enters trance by playing both hand drum (dharu) and a larger drum (nga) with long curved drum stick in right hand. *Photo by Larry Peters.*

■ **Figure 6-2.** Tilley, the son of Wangchuk, kneeling before the lama, Nyedon Rinpoche. *Photo by Larry Peters.*

■ **Figure 6-3.** The lamas performing the funeral rite. Reciting mantra. In front of the head lama is a cross-like structure holding photo of Wangchuk on the front, with his name written on the back. This will be burned, symbolizing the end of any remaining attachments Wangchuk may have to this life. *Photo by Larry Peters.*

■ **Figure 6-4.** The seated lama is Nyedon Rinpoche, who was in charge of administrating the 49-day rite. The walls of the entire room are lined with pictures of Buddhist deities and high-ranking incarnate lamas, adorned with ceremonial scarves of honor (khata). On the altar are torma, colorful offerings for the various deities. *Photo by Larry Peters.*

lakes, rivers, streams, waterfalls, wells, and the like. The retinue of spirit helpers of the lu include fish, frogs, and turtles. The lu may cause problems, as do the sten and other types of demons of the middle world, if they are not honored properly and consequently become defiled (dip). When they are defiled, they cause human illness of various types. Thus, like the ghosts and the demons, the lu too can be né pa, i.e., spirits that cause misfortune.

Refuge is recognized in the healing ritual when the shaman is fully costumed, which, for Rhichoe, is a long Tibetan jacket and, on top of that, a colorful, embroidered silk tunic and the five-lobed crown (rigs lnga). This is the moment when the shaman has become fully embodied by the deity's lights.

The red, fiery Sangri Sten, a srung mo, is the principal refuge deity of Rhichoe, whose lights and powers, and those of his retinue of spirits, work through Pau Rhichoe's body (refuge) during the healing ritual. A small picture of Sangri Sten is displayed second from the left on Pau Rhichoe's altar.

When completely costumed and drumming and sounding the loud hand bell, Rhichoe, embodied by the lights and powers of Sangri Sten, speaks to the illness-creating spirits (né pa) that have been called. He sees them along the corners of the lower mirror and in front of the altar, where offerings of rice have been left for them. An initial offering (*sergyum*) of water is made to them by the shaman's assistant. Pau Rhichoe says he then speaks to them "as if the two of us are having a discussion." He tells them to take refuge (devotion, in this context) in the Buddha, to give up their harmful ways, and to follow the deity's light to rebirth, and gets a promise that, if they take his self-sacrifice, they will stop bringing problems to the patient.

Rhichoe says that there are two types of dismemberment sacrifice (*chöd*): peaceful and wrathful. The peaceful sacrifice is the way the lama gives his body in their performance of chöd, like the compassionate Buddha did for a starving tiger and her emaciated cub as told in myth.

In the wrathful type, the né pa spirits (dre, shed, sten, etc.) come with their own weapons and tools and butcher the shaman. Rhichoe says that those that like the heart eat his heart, and others consume what they prefer. It is a banquet, a holy meal (*dur*) for the demons and ghosts, and they eat as we would do if we were very hungry. But it is dangerous. If something goes wrong in the rememberment, and the deity's light is not reabsorbed into the shaman's body (refuge), the shaman could die. It is because of the difficulty and danger involved that Pau Nyima does not use this method.

The né pa ghosts and demons, however, do not ingest the light. Rhichoe is not sure, but he thinks the deity's light goes into the sky, perhaps behind a cloud. Here it waits until the rememberment and then reunites with the reconstituted body of the shaman. Yet, the body that the né pa are given is a body transformed (gyur wa) and consecrated (rab né) by the deity's light and therefore a blessing for the hungry né pa spirits.

After the rememberment, the rest of the healing ritual follows. This may involve an extraction (jib), a shed phud, a la kuk (soul empowerment), and so forth.

The destiny of the né pa (spirits of misfortune) is varied. Some ghosts and demons may continue to attack the patient, in which case, the healing was not successful. Others merely temporarily satisfied by Pau Rhichoe's sacrifice may again cause problems to the same person at another time, or to different people. Still others might become stronger, thereby becoming lord or ruler of a particular place—for example, a graveyard—and demand propitiation. Another possibility is that the ghosts and demons will become better moral beings. Some ghosts may obey the shaman's advice and follow the lights to rebirth. After the dismemberment meal, those demons that have never taken birth, and are responsible for the patient's misfortune, are sent back to their "proper place." They are told by Pau Rhichoe, "You have received all you have asked, so return home and leave the patient alone."

When I discussed the same issue with a Buddhist rinpoché, he said that these nonhuman demons too can be helped and can be given an oath to be protectors of the faith and the faithful. They do not have srung mo status, as only those converted by Padma Sambhava himself are srung mo, but they can join the retinue of helping spirits of a srung mo and, in the process, support the *dharma* (doctrine) and the teachings of the compassionate Buddha, and no longer bring harm to other beings.

There is an old Tibetan saying that "A man died; a sten was born." Indeed, at death, a person's soul could become a sten, a powerful and wrathful middle world demon. Nyima says it could only happen to a very bad person.

However, as stated above, it all depends on the mental state of a person when he dies. Those who have been murdered, who die in fights, or who die in similar violent ways are likely the most "attached" to vengeful and hateful thoughts and, after death, their rage could take a demonic form, and bring harm to human life. In other words, the capacity of the heart determines the destiny of the soul.

CONCLUSION

The new data presented here, in some respects, clarifies my previous writings on the subject, and is important, as it shows large areas of the cultural and spiritual coherence of Buddhism and shamanism. Traditionally, this takes form in the cooperative community fire ceremony, albeit at the camp ritual the elder shamans did not participate,[38] but especially in the compassionate attitude taken toward the ghosts. The Living Treasure Nyima says, "We do not just throw them, but try to help them find the light to rebirth."

Thus it seems that shamanic healing rituals have many distinct elements. But, among the purposes of shamanic rituals, similar to the lama rituals for the dead, is to psychopomp or guide the soul to a rebirth.

Often this has been thought to be entirely the cultural function of the lama. This is not so; shamans also do this work. Thus their healings treat the patient but, at the same time, assist the ghosts to turn from doing harm, follow the light, and leave the bardo by taking a rebirth.

REFERENCES

Eliade, Mircea. *Shamanism.* Princeton, NJ: Princeton University Press, 1964.

Peters, Larry G. "The *Ghe-wa* (Tibetan Death Rite) for Pau Karma Wangchuk Namgyal," *Shamanism Annual* 21 (2008): 2–7.

———. "Tradition, Practice, and Trance of the Foundation's Tibetan Living Treasures." *Shamanism Annual* 22 (2010): 2–19.

Sifers, Sarah. *Fate of the Lhapa* (film). Watertown, MA: Documentary Educational Resources, 2008.

· 4 ·

THE TIBETAN HEALING RITUALS *of* DORJE YÜDRONMA

A Fierce Manifestation of Feminine Cosmic Force

Boudha (literally Lord Buddha) is a unique community outside Kathmandu with a long history as a Tibetan Buddhist pilgrimage site because of its enormous towering *stupa* (reliquary shrine). The area literally teems with tourists who come by bus and taxi through the day, seven days a week, to see the stupa. Frequently called "Little Tibet"—because most of its inhabitants trace their ancestry to Tibet—Boudha has grown enormously in the twenty years since I first began anthropological fieldwork there. Due to large-scale development and population influxes from outlying areas, there is now hardly an open space in the six miles between Boudha and Kathmandu. Curio shops abound, along with Tibetan carpet factories, restaurants, guesthouses, and a bustling bazaar where local folks sell everything needed to maintain a household.

Although Boudha is home to a multiethnic community, a high percentage of its residents are Tamang (a Tibetan ethnic group that has resided for centuries in the Himalaya mountains separating Tibet and Nepal). Moreover, since the Chinese occupation of Tibet in the 1950s, many Tibetan refugees have settled in Boudha, and they have become a dominant cultural force in the area. There are at least a dozen active monasteries, representing all of the Tibetan Buddhist sects. Tibetan medicine is practiced alongside numerous other healing methods, including shamanism.

During my four-and-a-half-month visit to Boudha in 1996, I had the opportunity to meet and observe a very dramatic and powerful Tibetan healer, who is known both by the lay name Mrs. Dolkar and by the spiritual title of Lhamo. A lhamo (*lha* = deity; *mo* = female) is a type of traditional Tibetan oracle who can temporarily embody deities who enable her to perform shamanic healing and divination work. A Tibetan refugee who has lived in the Boudha area for several years, Mrs. Dolkar is recognized as the lhamo who manifests the divine healer and protector Dorje Yüdronma, a mountain deity incorporated into Buddhism after Padma Sambhava brought Buddhism to Tibet.

Mrs. Dolkar has been officially "certified" by H. H. the Dalai Lama as a "reliable exorcist" for "all mental and physical ills and problems."[39] However, as His Holiness notes in a fascinating one-paragraph document, Mrs. Dolkar was once considered a "wild schizophrenic" who was "possessed" by occult powers. It was only after she was purified, initiated, and trained by another lhamo that she became the "possessor" of the Goddess Dorje Yüdronma—"a shamanic manifestation of cosmic force."

Mrs. Dolkar's path to becoming a lhamo was a long and traumatic journey.[40] Because no one in her family was a shaman (which was the case with other Tibetan shamans I interviewed), she did not have the benefit of an experienced teacher to guide her as a child. When she was initially "chosen" by the Goddess, she didn't know what was happening and she became very ill. As a child, she suffered violent fits and exhibited psychotic behavior, and it wasn't until years later, after she learned to embody the Goddess, that she was healed and became a healer.

At the age of thirteen, she became a Buddhist nun in Tibet, where she spent her adolescence. By her own account, people called her "Crazy Nun," because her behavior was so erratic and unstable. She could be kind and generous—occasionally even giving away her clothes to needy people in the street—but she was also prone to angry outbursts and violent episodes.

While still a young nun, she had a series of dreams and visions that she felt compelled to literally follow. In these dreams, a mysterious old woman told her that she must go to live in a strange land where she did not know the customs or language, and where she would meet H. H. the Dalai Lama. The woman in the dreams persuaded her to leave the nunnery without telling anyone, advising her that secrecy was best for all concerned. The young nun obeyed and followed the old woman, traveling only at night, trekking over high mountain passes, and resting in caves during the day, as she was directed. The mysterious guide, who seemed to need neither food nor drink nor sleep, would appear each night with food for the girl and would then lead her on the night's journey, only to vanish magically during the day. The journey lasted for three days, by which time the young girl was too far from home to turn back. Still in Tibet and without the old guide, she found work as a washerwoman. It was then that she met and married her first husband, with whom she eventually moved to India, where, at the age of twenty-three, she had a son.

She lived in India for many years. After leaving her first husband, she considered returning to Tibet. However, the mysterious old woman reappeared in her dreams and guided her to Calcutta, where she met her present husband, Mr. Dolkar ("Pala"), who now assists at her rituals. Despite a happy marriage, Mrs. Dolkar continued to experience violent episodes, sometimes assaulting people or destroying property (even her family's possessions). She experienced hallucinations—some frightening, others divine. Her behavior was so erratic that people decided that she was beset by evil spirits. From time to time, she went on pilgrimages to visit great lamas for blessings and healings. Sometimes, it seemed she was improving, but then the episodes would return. Her behavior was so unpredictable that she was unable to hold down a job, and Pala was prevented from continuing his own career as a restaurant owner and cook. To make matters worse, her son became mentally disturbed at age thirteen—"just like me," she says—and began manifesting symptoms similar to those she had experienced as a youngster in Tibet.

Unable to find steady work, the Dolkars moved around a lot, living in Bodgaya, Calcutta, Delhi, and Kathmandu before emigrating to Ladakh about fourteen years ago. In Ladakh, the lama Taklung Tsetrul Rinpoche and a fierce divine-incarnate healer named Saphod Lhamo (affectionately known as Abhi Lhamo) both recognized Mrs. Dolkar's shamanic potential. While receiving healings from Abhi Lhamo, Mrs. Dolkar began to demonstrate certain psychic and healing abilities typical of a lhamo. Abhi Lhamo divined that Mrs. Dolkar had been chosen by the Goddess Dorje Yüdronma because she had been the Goddess's faithful devotee in a previous life. Abhi Lhamo believed that Mrs. Dolkar's mental difficulties were due to the fact that her veins or channels (tsa) were "unclear" and "unclean," which prevented the Goddess from fully entering her.

For a year and a half, Abhi Lhamo was Mrs. Dolkar's healer and guru. After undergoing a series of Abhi Lhamo's sometimes-brutal healings with a bamboo pole, Mrs. Dolkar was eventually purified and made ready to receive the Goddess. Mrs. Dolkar says she is very grateful for Abhi Lhamo's healings, which made it possible for her to bring the Goddess into her in a controlled manner. Now that she has learned how to open herself to the Goddess in a ritual context, she is no longer subjected to the involuntary possessions that had caused her such suffering.

Eventually, Abhi Lhamo began to test Mrs. Dolkar's skills as a healer. In one case, Mrs. Dolkar healed Abhi Lhamo's grandchild. In another, she extracted a nail from the throat of a sick yak. Despite certain similarities, Mrs. Dolkar's healings turned out to be significantly different from those of her guru. Unlike Abhi Lhamo's rituals, which generally involved beatings with a bamboo pole and only infrequently used sucking extractions, Mrs. Dolkar's healings incorporated various other forms of exorcism and often involved sucking extractions. Mrs.

Dolkar says that everything that happens in her rituals, from divination to sucking, arises "automatically," i.e., of its own accord (see Figures 4-1 and 4-2).

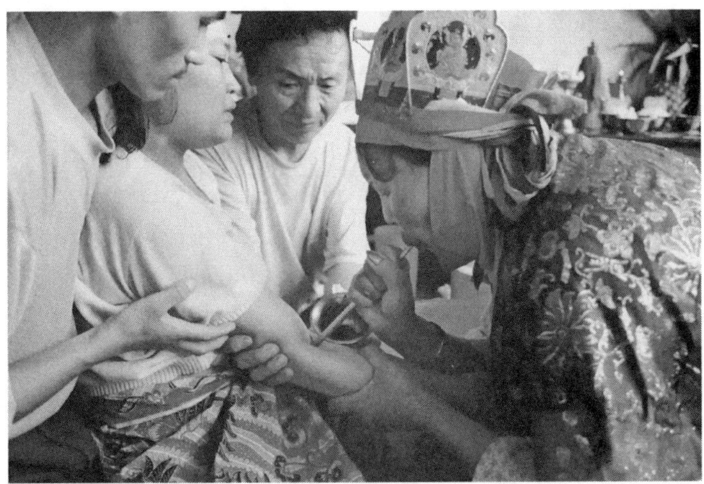

Figure 4-1. Dorje Yüdronma sucks an illness from a patient.
Photo by Larry Peters.

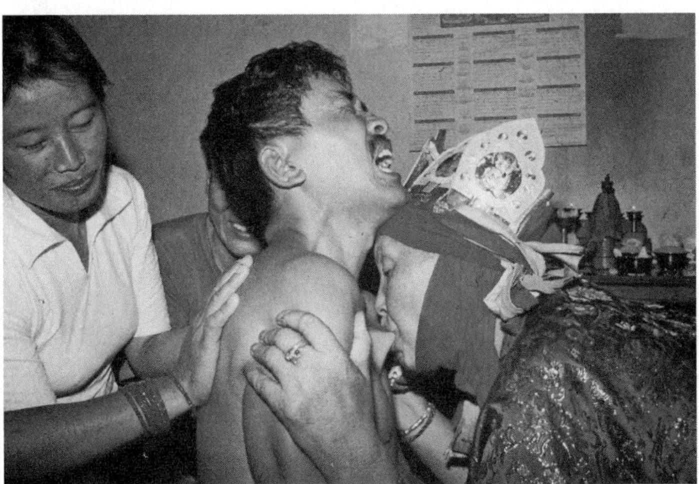

Figure 4-2. Lhamo's healing work involves a combination of shamanic extraction and painfully vigorous spiritual exorcism.
Photo by Larry Peters.

Mrs. Dolkar's authenticity as a divine oracle was also put to the test. At one session, after Mrs. Dolkar became possessed, Abhi Lhamo asked who it was that was embodying her, and Mrs. Dolkar replied she was Dorje Yüdronma. The Goddess then related a detailed story about how she had left Tibet long ago—knowing that enemies would invade her country—and had settled on a mountaintop in Ladakh, where she had built a monastery. Still under trance possession, Mrs. Dolkar described the monastery as it had been long ago and explained that it had since fallen into ruins—its precious objects had been stolen, and a pond containing healing waters had been destroyed. Although such revelations are not unusual in Tibetan Buddhist tradition, their authenticity is often put to the test. A search party was sent to find the monastery based on the description Mrs. Dolkar had given in trance. Although the monastery proved very difficult to locate, its remains were discovered, and all saw that it was as Mrs. Dolkar had described. Having passed that test, Mrs. Dolkar was formally recognized and ordained by Abhi Lhamo and Taklung Tsetrul Rinpoche. From that time on, Mrs. Dolkar has been accepted as the Goddess's oracle.

Gradually, Mrs. Dolkar's fame spread, and H. H. the Dalai Lama asked her to come to his residence at Dharamsala, India, to perform a healing. She did and it was successful. While in Dharamsala, Mrs. Dolkar also attended a trance performance of the Nechung State Oracle. When the Nechung oracle experienced some difficulties during his performance, Mrs. Dolkar spontaneously embodied the Goddess and helped him. Later, she had an audience with H. H. the Dalai Lama, who agreed to write a letter acknowledging her abilities (see note 1). Mrs. Dolkar proudly displays his letter over her altar.

Mrs. Dolkar's healing was her initiation, and her initiation was her healing. Her psychotic-like episodes have not reappeared during the seven years since she developed spiritual intimacy with the Goddess. Some people might be tempted to argue that the rapid change in her social role and status—from being treated as a disturbed individual to being respected as an incarnate deity and healer—could have prompted a change in her psychological condition. Mrs. Dolkar prefers to credit the healing to her guru and the Goddess. Whatever the cause, her explosive anger and violent behavior are now circumscribed into her divine role in ritual, where they have been sublimated and harnessed for purposes of healing and community service. Interestingly, Mrs. Dolkar takes little personal credit for her healings: she humbly insists that she is only a channel and that whatever happens during her rituals comes directly from the Goddess.

A VIOLENT BUT COMPASSIONATE HEALER

The drama of Lhamo's healing rituals is enhanced by an element of paradox. On the one hand, when patients first arrive, they are greeted warmly by the Dolkars and treated to an atmosphere of relaxed cordiality. Mrs. Dolkar is charming, and most people feel welcome. Before the ritual begins, Pala goes to great lengths to make sure everyone is comfortable, providing cushions and serving a choice of teas and biscuits. Lhamo often tells a joke and puts her patients at ease before the magic and violence fill the air.

Unlike the renowned Nechung oracle and other monastic oracle-priests who are possessed by the highest-ranking deities (*ch'ökyong*) of the Buddhist pantheon, most lhamo and their male counterparts, lhapa, are lay practitioners who usually embody a lower class of fierce protective deities (*srungma*) associated with Tibetan pre-Buddhist Bön shamanism. In another difference from oracle-priests, who primarily serve monastic orders, most lhamo and lhapa hold séances in their own or others' homes, and they help ordinary people find solutions to day-to-day problems.

The protective deities embodied by lhamo and lhapa tend to exhibit both fierce and compassionate natures. For example, the deity that Lhamo embodies, Dorje Yüdronma, is recognized in Tibetan

Buddhism as having two appearances (Nebesky-Wojkowitz 1993, 191). Her most common form is a lustrous white crystalline being, but she also has a fierce black aspect, which drips blood from its mouth and issues fire from its eyes and smoke from its nostrils.

In keeping with the nature of the Goddess she embodies, Lhamo's healing rituals are incredibly dramatic affairs, involving a unique mixture of sympathetic concern and fiercely brutal and painful procedures. Mrs. Dolkar herself is a kind, warm, and gentle sixty-two-year-old woman—at least when she is not embodying the Goddess. However, when Lhamo launches into the fierce shamanic performances that bear the unmistakable signature of the Goddess Dorje Yüdronma, she can provoke real fear in her patients.

Standing about five feet ten inches tall and weighing around 160 pounds, Mrs. Dolkar is a big woman by Asian standards and a formidable force when inspired by the Goddess (see Figure 4-3). I have seen Lhamo beat her patients, grab their hair, slap their faces, and hit them soundly with her fists on their chests, backs, and shoulders. She may forcefully and repeatedly throw holy water in their faces at point-blank range, or she may purposely spit in their faces and mouths, all the while repeating various mantra for healing. Sometimes she rubs the blood taken from the Goddess's mouth onto their faces and bodies.

However, Lhamo is best known as a "sucking doctor" who heals by extracting poisons, polluted substances, and other objects from her patients' bodies. Lhamo has many of her clients partially undress, and then she sucks and bites them forcefully on the shoulders, chest, stomach, thighs, and feet. She bites hard, leaving deep tooth marks. Interestingly, although the Goddess occasionally bites herself to draw her own blood as a medicine for a patient, I never saw her bites break her patients' skin. Sometimes she sucks through a thin, foot-long copper straw that she literally jams into a patient's flesh. Eventually, Lhamo spits out the items that she has extracted from the patient. I have seen her remove large pieces of rotten, putrid meat; globs of

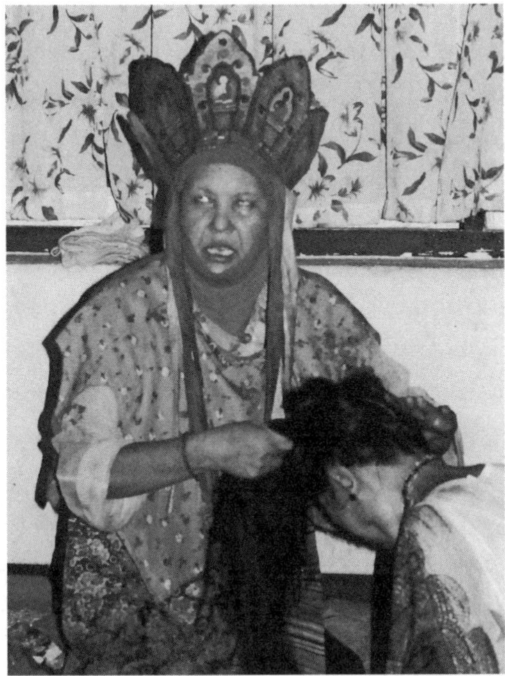

Figure 4-3. Mrs. Dolkar is a big woman, making her a formidable force when she embodies the Goddess. Photo by Larry Peters.

black, tar-like "blood"; yellow, murky liquid; balls of hair; black or white stones; nails; and a worm.

While some observers may be tempted to discount these techniques as theatrical displays designed to amaze and impress those waiting to be healed, most patients testify that they undergo Lhamo's healings only because they work. The extractions are very painful procedures, often leaving red marks that later turn into black-and-blue bruises. While I have observed many other Tibetan and Nepali shamans perform similar extraction techniques, their extractions have tended to be remarkably mild and painless compared to Lhamo's violent methods. It is not unusual for Lhamo's patients to scream out that they are about to die and to plead with her to stop.

Although I am an anthropologist with a strong sense of "cultural relativism," I initially viewed Lhamo's violent healing work with some distrust and confusion. I understood that in Hindu and Buddhist cosmologies, the sacred often contains antithetical aspects: divine aspects of wisdom and compassion tend to be paired with fierce aspects, which may appear repulsive and threatening to the uninitiated. However, I still had difficulty understanding the therapeutic usefulness of physically hurting one's patients. Eventually, as I came to know her, I began to see how Lhamo's healings worked from within the local cultural paradigms.

Striking patients is a fairly common practice in Nepal, at least among many of the shamans I have observed. Both the shamans and their patients view these attacks as exorcistic techniques directed against the demons and other evil spirits that are causing the illness or pain. Because people see the interventions as helpful blessings coming from the Goddess—not as personal attacks on their bodies and minds—patients accept the violence as an integral part of the treatments, and they voluntarily submit to the techniques.

Lhamo, like many other Tibetan protective deities, may appear to be fierce and violent, but her essential nature is the embodiment of compassion. Although Lhamo typically inflicts violent treatments on everyone who comes to her—including high-ranking lama and even Westerners—she is remarkably gentle with children. Mrs. Dolkar is devoted to relieving the suffering of others, and Lhamo's violent methods appear to be directed at provoking a spiritual crisis in order to bring about a healing in her patients. Certainly, if Lhamo's work is any indication, such drastic practices can be therapeutic.

TRANCE MEDIUMS OR SHAMANIC VISIONARIES

Although there has been some debate in scholarly circles as to whether Tibetan trance oracles such as lhamo and lhapa tend to describe their trance methodology primarily in terms of "embodying spirits" or undergoing "trance possessions" (as opposed to making ecstatic soul flights), a case can be made that these folk oracles not only perform shamanistic healing procedures but also enter shamanic trance states.

Many scholars—including Mircea Eliade (1964) and Michael Harner (1990)—consider ecstatic "soul flights" to be the principal defining trait of the shaman's trance. Both Eliade and Harner argue that the shaman's trance—or ecstasy—involves a "magical flight" or journeying of the soul, allowing shamans to see and participate in an ordinarily hidden spiritual, or "nonordinary," reality. As Sandra Ingerman (1991) suggests, shamans may also "see" through other senses, as well as through visions.

First of all, it should be mentioned that there are numerous accounts in Tibetan mythology and literature that indicate that shamanic techniques of ecstatic soul flight once played an important role in Tibet, particularly before its conversion to Buddhism began about a thousand years ago (Norbu 1995, 283f.). Eliade (1964, 436–441, 506–507) notes that many of the archaic pre-Buddhist rites, deities, and practices of Tibetan shamanism were incorporated into Tantric Buddhism, but he argues they were converted or changed in the process. Because Buddhist meditation stresses "embodiment," and Buddhist philosophy rejects the reality of the soul (*anatma*), Eliade suggests that the shamanic techniques of ecstatic soul flight were reevaluated and changed. Even if one assumes the devaluation of shamanic practices in orthodox Buddhist philosophy, Geoffrey Samuel (1993) notes that pre-Buddhist shamanic practices have been preserved in Tibetan folk religion particularly in conservative regions geographically removed from the great monastic complexes. Furthermore, shamanic soul journeying is still practiced among many of the Tibetan ethnic groups residing in the Himalayan regions of Nepal (Holmberg 1989; Mumford 1989; Peters 1981; Sagant 1996).

After having observed a great many of Lhamo's healing séances, I am convinced that the soul journeys and visioning play a significant role in her trance healings. The first time I witnessed Lhamo's journeying process, she was treating a young woman who was weak and quite thin. Lhamo unexpectedly collapsed in front of her altar and lay motionless alongside her patient for three or four minutes. I was completely surprised. She was curled on her side in a fetal position. When I noticed she was turning blue, my first thought was that she was choking on something she had sucked out of her patient, and I prepared to perform the Heimlich maneuver to dislodge it. Then, in an instant, she sprang up—with her drum in one hand and a handful of wheat used for divination in the other. Without missing a beat, she tossed the wheat on the drum and determined that her journey was successful.

Mrs. Dolkar later explained that the Goddess had left her body and traveled to a place near Boudha, where the patient had earlier been attacked by harmful spirits. She said that, because the case was serious and there wasn't time for the patient to perform the sacrifice herself, the Goddess had gone to the spot and performed a goat sacrifice to placate the harmful spirits that had caused the illness. In other words, Lhamo, while lying on the ground, had initiated an ecstatic journey and enacted the sacrifice in nonordinary reality.

Lhamo also "sees" in other shamanistic ways. In a procedure remarkably similar to that used in many traditions of Siberian shamanism, Lhamo will look into a mirror to divine the causes of a patient's illness and the appropriate spiritual remedies. In addition, she frequently makes use of her uncanny clairvoyant abilities during healings.

Although Mrs. Dolkar describes her séances primarily in terms of "spirit embodiment" or "trance possession," these terms should not be confused with dissociative possessions. Her trance possession starts and ends at will—it is a controlled trance. As the British social anthropologist I. M. Lewis (1989) suggests, the voluntary control of trance states through ceremonial ritual is a vital feature distinguishing shamanic trances from dissociative or demonic possessions. It is worth noting that the language used by H. H. the Dalai Lama to describe Mrs. Dolkar's controlled trance possessions is remarkably similar to the terminology used by the Russian ethnographer S. M. Shirokogoroff (1935), who observed that Siberian Tungus shamans are not "possessed" but are the "possessors" of the spirits.

Another vital characteristic of shamanic trance is that the shaman can remember the trance experience (Peters and Price-Williams 1980). Even though Mrs. Dolkar claims to be amnesic, as might be expected in Tibetan culture, she actually seems to remember quite a bit of what happens. Often, when I was unclear about some aspect of a healing, Mrs. Dolkar was able to tell me what the Goddess had said or thought about the patient's illness. Moreover, as the above case makes clear, she can remember the Goddess's "soul journeys."

It seems that Mrs. Dolkar's dissociative states, if there are any, are limited to the extractions Lhamo performs. Mrs. Dolkar considers the substances Lhamo extracts from patients to be *jutho* (spiritually polluted). Once when I showed her pictures I had taken of Lhamo sucking and biting a patient, Mrs. Dolkar became very angry and turned her head away, saying that the photos made her ill. Tearfully, she questioned why the Goddess had chosen her to do such unclean work, reiterating that the extracted blood and meat were disgusting. It seems to me that she did not like talking about this aspect of her work, not that she didn't remember it.

Lhamo's healing work involves another element with parallels to the classic shamanic model. Mrs. Dolkar says that, during healing rituals, she often embodies different deities as needed for different healing procedures. The second most important deity that she embodies is Kyi-tra-pala, a ferocious guardian dog deity (see Figure 4-4). He is one of a class of deities called srungma, who watch over temples and other sacred places, as well as over persons and even some other deities. Frequently, Tibetan shamans will work with one or more srungma (Berglie 1976), which appear to be analogous in some respects to "power animals" in other shamanic traditions (see Nebesky-Wojkowitz 1993, 481–483).

The dog deity Kyi-tra-pala is the srungma of Taklung Tsetrul Rinpoche's monastery. Kyi-tra-pala serves Lhamo by removing polluted

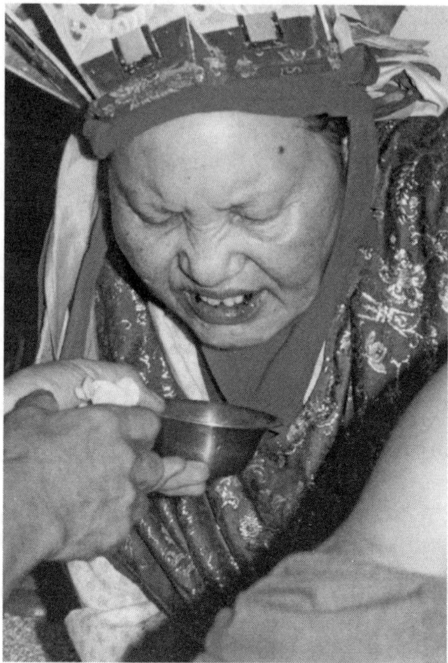

Figure 4-4. Mrs. Dolkar often embodies the dog deity Kyi-tra- pala when performing extractions. Photo by Larry Peters.

substances from her patients. Mrs. Dolkar says that she embodies this powerful protective divinity whenever she sucks and bites a patient. It not only attacks and chases away the afflicting spirits, but it extracts their polluted creations at the same time. Indeed, when Mrs. Dolkar performs an extraction, she often snaps and growls like a fierce dog. During healings, the passage of identities from Lhamo to Kyi-tra-pala, and vice versa, occurs without any noticeable event. One moment the dog deity is embodied; the next, Lhamo is explaining to the patient the meaning of what was extracted.

Another nearly universal magical ability of shamans (although not limited to shamans) is their "mastery over fire" (Eliade 1964, 412). I found it very interesting that, one evening each week, Lhamo conducts a "fire ceremony" to which she invites any patients from her previous six morning healing sessions who she feels might benefit (usually those who were treated for possession or who were suffering from serious illnesses). As might be expected, the ritual room is frequently crowded with patients (see Figure 4-5).

The fire ceremony centers around a huge copper pot filled with paper, wood, and coals, all of which are doused with flammable liquid and then set ablaze. Flames shoot up from the cauldron, and heat quickly fills the closed, unventilated room. Despite the heat, Lhamo sits close to the fire in full ritual attire.

As each patient takes a turn sitting before her, near the pot, Lhamo waves her hands through the flames and puts her face close to the fire. She seems to swallow the flames, and then she slaps and spits on the face, bare shoulders, legs, and torso of each patient until all have been treated with the healing fire. This portion of the fire ceremony can take up to an hour, and it can be a trial just to stay in the room, especially on a hot, muggy evening. Although Lhamo spends the entire session hovering over the flames or sitting next to the hot copper pot,

Figure 4-5. During a fire ceremony, Lhamo hovers for long periods over a flaming cauldron, demonstrating her shamanic mastery over fire. Photo by Larry Peters.

she appears to be undisturbed by the heat. Lhamo's mastery over heat and fire is just one of her magical abilities that defy "physical laws" and affirm her role as a shaman and deity.

INVOKING THE GODDESS

Mrs. Dolkar's healing séances invariably begin with the performance of a sacramental ritual process used to induce a trance state and invoke the presence of the Goddess. As Mrs. Dolkar stands in the corner of her ritual room, facing toward her altar on the opposite wall, Pala envelops her body with smoke from a bowl of burning sage. The altar, which is about fifteen feet away, is adorned with ritual paraphernalia and pictures of lama, including one of H. H. the Dalai Lama. A *thangka* (ritual painting) of the White Tara hangs on the wall above and to the left side of the altar.

After being thoroughly cleansed by the incense, Mrs. Dolkar begins to pray and repeatedly prostrates herself, moving gradually across the room. As she approaches the altar, her eyes roll progressively upward and she yawns, snorts, hiccups, laughs loudly, and sneezes—all signs that the Goddess is announcing herself. Once manifested, Lhamo stands before her audience of patients and their supporters. There may be as few as a half dozen or as many as twenty-five people. She picks up a two-foot-long sword and pounds her chest with it several times. Then she motions threateningly with it at the audience. Sometimes she moves among the assemblage, lightly striking individuals with the sword. Eventually, she sits before the altar and dons her ritual clothes, completing the process of personal transformation and Goddess embodiment.

Mrs. Dolkar explains that, before she can put on her ritual garb, her soul must leave her body and go to rest in the flaming white mirror depicted in the thangka of Tara. At the same time that her own soul passes into the thangka, Dorje Yüdronma reveals herself from behind Tara and comes through the thangka to occupy Mrs. Dolkar's body.

During this embodiment process—after her soul has left and the Goddess has yet to arrive—Mrs. Dolkar's body leans motionless against the wall for a moment.

Similarly, at the close of the day's healings, when the Goddess leaves and Mrs. Dolkar's soul returns, her body collapses momentarily in front of the altar. Whenever Mrs. Dolkar's body is temporarily left without a soul, as when the Goddess journeyed to make a goat sacrifice for a patient, she collapses and lies completely still on the ground until the Goddess returns to her body.

The foremost part of Lhamo's ritual garb is the five-pointed lama's crown (ringa) depicting the five *Dhyana,* or meditation Buddhas. These Dhyana represent many aspects of Tibetan Buddhist cosmology (Govinda 1969), including the five directions, five elements, and five chakra. Lhamo also wears a red cloth skullcap, a blue cape of embroidered silk, and a red cloth mouth cover similar to a surgeon's mask. Whenever she does extractions, the mouth cover is pushed down under her chin (see Figure 4-6).

Once Lhamo is fully attired, she rings a Tibetan ritual bell (*drilbu*) loudly with her left hand while twirling a small hand drum (*dhamaru*) in her right. In addition to these loud, rhythmic sounds, Lhamo begins chanting in a shrill but captivating voice for three or four minutes. Simultaneously, she uses a small ritual silver spoon—held deftly in her left hand alongside the bell—to toss milk from a silver bowl on the altar as offerings for the deities and spirits.

Once the deity is fully embodied, patients take turns approaching the altar before which Lhamo sits. Although these séances provide laypeople with a unique opportunity to meet deity face-to-face—and spectacular events sometimes occur as the deities make themselves manifest—their primary function is to provide spiritual healing and practical help with day-to-day problems. Lhamo feels their pulse and asks what is wrong. Sometimes she does a preliminary divination using her drum, after which the treatment begins in earnest.

Figure 4-6. When treating illnesses caused by spirit possession, Lhamo often uses violent assaults and extractions to scare away the offending spirits. Photo by Larry Peters.

During the healings, those not being treated often speak with each other, telling of people they know who have received healings from Lhamo. Most patients clearly admire the Goddess and her work, and this creates an air of awe and sanctity in the room. Lhamo dominates all activity, threatening violence if she is not obeyed at once. Lhamo is fierce, and she is feared. She is also honored.

THE EXORCISM OF HARMFUL SPIRITS

Lhamo is a versatile healer who has a reputation for being able to treat nearly every type of illness: spiritual or physical, mild or severe. In some cases, after her ritual diagnosis, Lhamo will advise a patient to consult a doctor in order to get help for the physical aspects of a disorder. Sometimes she recommends herbs or vitamins for patients to complement her shamanic healing. Occasionally she performs small operations, such as using a razor blade to remove a wart. However, whenever the oracle indicates a patient's symptoms are the result of spirit possession or attack—which is most of the time—Lhamo's healing work involves a combination of shamanic extraction and spiritual exorcism.

One of the most interesting healings I observed involved a middle-aged Nepalese woman who walked into Lhamo's room on the sides of her feet. As the patient sat down in front of Lhamo's altar, she began to shake (the cultural idiom for possession); this was one of three cases involving trance possession that I observed. Despite the shaking, everyone's attention turned to the patient's feet, which were curled and twisted. Lhamo jammed her *phurba* (ritual dagger) into the bottoms of the woman's feet over and over. The patient, or rather the *bokshi* (usually translated as "witch") possessing her, screamed. Holding the phurba firmly against the patient's foot, Lhamo sucked on the handle of the dagger.

Lhamo appeared to be beating the bokshi out of the patient and extracting poisons from her body through sucking. The bokshi spoke, but no one understood; it sounded like glossolalia to me. For a half hour, the woman's husband and daughter affectionately attended to her while she recovered at the back of the room. After resting, the patient walked out unaided on straight feet.

This patient was asked to return in five days for a fire ceremony. On the appointed evening, on my way to Lhamo's, I saw the patient and her family. Her gait seemed relatively normal. However, as she reached Lhamo's door—the door to the ritual room—her feet suddenly turned inward, and she was again unable to walk. She screamed and began to curse while she waited in the ritual room with her husband, brother, and daughter.

After the fire was lit in front of Lhamo's altar, Lhamo began working on the woman's feet, straightening them out and having her get up and down. She sucked on the feet through her phurba, spitting out chunks of meat and blood. The patient screamed that she was going to die, that the pain was too great. But Lhamo persisted, demanding that the bokshi possessing the patient make itself known. Using the threat of the fire and the phurba, Lhamo forced the bokshi to capitulate, and it confessed to "telling lies" and to "betraying others." Lhamo made the bokshi promise to leave the patient and cause no further problems.

In my only discussion with the patient and her husband, I was told that the symptoms of seizures, twisting of the feet, and speaking strangely had begun six years earlier. The woman had been given a brain scan and was diagnosed by physicians as having a brain dysfunction. However, none of the doctors consulted had been able to help, so the family had come to Lhamo as a last resort. I tried in vain to arrange a meeting with this patient before I left Nepal, in order to verify her story and the results of the healing. However, three months after Lhamo's exorcism, my field assistant spoke with the patient and with Mrs. Dolkar, and both reported that the patient was without further episodes.

A CURE FOR ALCOHOLISM

Over the course of my visit, I observed Lhamo treating numerous alcoholics, and these treatments always followed the same pattern. First, Lhamo would suck the patient's stomach, chest, and neck at least once; then she would drop grains of wheat onto her drum to determine if additional sucking was needed. Each patient had been required to bring in a small bottle filled with liquor. Lhamo would spit a goodly amount of her blood into the bottle, and then she would insist that the patient drink it. If there was any resistance, she would slap the patient's face and body until he or she complied. Sometimes she would beat the patient with her sword. Lhamo does not take "no" for an answer.

When I later asked Mrs. Dolkar to explain why she has the patients drink the blood, her husband explained that the Goddess uses her blood as a medicine for the patient. This blood is considered holy and beneficial—just the opposite of the extracted blood, which is considered polluted.

One alcoholic patient was brought to Lhamo by a friend who had just completed his master's degree in sociology. The friend mentioned to me that he had brought many patients to Lhamo and that she had helped some of them, including himself. He said he had lost his taste for alcohol since drinking the Goddess's blood.

VIOLENT BLESSINGS OF THE GODDESS

One of Lhamo's most dramatic and violent treatments that I observed was given to a wealthy, thirty-three-year-old Nepalese man. He came to Lhamo's house with his wife and five-year-old son, and they were all impeccably dressed in Western style. The man had been forced to resign from a lucrative job in another country because he had taken ill. He related that his throat felt as if it was being "scratched by a cat's nails," and that he shook. He had been brought to see Lhamo because he had been chronically angry at his wife and children, without reason, since his return home.

Lhamo violently sucked meat and blood out of his stomach and throat, causing him to cry out. Then the Goddess became more brutal than I had previously witnessed. She slapped and hit him numerous times. She threw volleys of water at his face at point-blank range. She did not bother putting a bib over his handsome clothes, as she generally does for patients, and she demanded that he keep his eyes and mouth open. Over and over, she doused the man with water until, out of pity, Pala began putting smaller amounts of water in her ritual bowl. Lhamo noticed and slapped Pala across the face with the bowl, demanding the full amount. She resumed the process of drowning the patient, who was soaked to the skin, shaking, and screaming at the top of his lungs.

Lhamo demanded to know the name of the spirit possessing the patient. At first, no one could understand the man's screams. Lhamo said they were in a foreign language. Then the spirit identified itself as the hundred-and-eight-year-old grandmother of a woman friend. That was all the man said, and then he began to scream again. Lhamo appeared determined to break him down. The more he screamed, the more she hit him. She said that the man was possessed by a bokshi and that she was trying to drive it out of him. The patient responded by crying and shaking more. Finally, Lhamo had the man moved to the back of the room, where he lay down on a cot and quieted down. However, in a few minutes, he began screaming again.

Lhamo had already started working on the next patient, but she stopped the healing. She went over to the screaming man and pounded him on the chest with her fist. "No good bokshi!" she screamed. Then she stood and put the full force of her foot on his chest. She threatened to do so on his throat. She ordered Pala to get a scrap of meat from their garbage, from the previous night's dinner, and she shoved it into the patient's mouth as an insult to the bokshi. Finally, the man quieted down, but he had to be helped into his car, and a driver had to be called to come and drive the car home.

Later, Pala and Lhamo's niece explained to me that this man had been possessed by a bokshi while he was abroad and that it was the bokshi who had made him ill and who was screaming and speaking in a foreign language during the healing. When the patient returned for a second treatment, Lhamo unearthed that he had been "spoiled" by the woman friend, the granddaughter of the bokshi. Lhamo asked if the woman had given him anything or taken anything of his, and he replied that she had given him two pillows and a locket that he was wearing around his neck. Lhamo asked him to take the locket off, and she pried it open with a knife. When she found strands of hair inside, Lhamo announced it was "love magic." The patient confessed to having had an affair with the woman. Apparently his wife already knew of it. Lhamo said the patient had lost his will to the bokshi's power. She added that the man's *karma* was very bad, which was why he was so vulnerable. She said that the only reason he had been doing well financially was because his wife was favored by the spirits.

When the man returned for the fire ceremony, he brought the two pillows and left them with Lhamo. Lhamo warned him not to speak with the woman if she called on the phone, and she suggested that he let his wife answer all phone calls for a month or two. Above all, she admonished him to keep his "bed clean." The treatment seemed to be directed toward breaking the woman's connection to the man and to restoring the family equilibrium.

About two months later, when I visited this patient at his home in Nepal, I learned that he had been well for about six weeks, but that recently he had begun shaking again. He said that otherwise he was feeling much better than before; he was no longer angry at his wife and children, and he was actually enjoying his stay at home. As we spoke, he confided that he had been contemplating returning to work, which would involve leaving Nepal and going back to where all his troubles had begun. When I asked what Lhamo thought of his plans, he said he had been going to a new healer. He believed that Lhamo was a great healer and that she could have healed him, but he had been afraid of being beaten again. When I discussed the case with Mrs. Dolkar, she said she felt bad that she had hurt him during the healing, but she contended that those beaten the worst by the Goddess actually receive the greatest blessing.

While Lhamo often tends to be generous with her violent blessings, particularly with adults, there are some exceptions to the rule. I observed an interesting session with a young Western patient, a female student who was spending a semester abroad with her college class. While watching Lhamo heal another patient, this young woman began to shake. Instead of beating the girl—Lhamo's typical treatment for shaking—she embraced and kissed her. While still holding her firmly, Lhamo told her that she was the daughter of a sacred Serpent King spirit and that she had mystical powers. This intervention ended the seizure immediately. Lhamo let her rest in her bedroom afterward. Later, the young student mentioned that she'd experienced the shaking before, and that the incident might have been triggered by watching Lhamo's extractions.

Lhamo's healing rituals can certainly be intensely dramatic affairs, not only because of the fierce and violent techniques used in her exorcisms, but also because she can be a disconcertingly accurate oracle when it comes to uncovering the circumstances surrounding a person's illness. As I watched her work nearly every day for several weeks, I was struck by her ability to divine key information about each patient and by the fact that amazing synchronicities became commonplace occurrences during her rituals. I was even more impressed by the way her healings worked on patients who did not understand her system, or who rejected it because of conflicting cultural paradigms.

TREATING SKEPTICS AND NONBELIEVERS

While it may be tempting to attribute the efficacy of Lhamo's healings to the power of cultural paradigms and hypnotic suggestion, I saw that Lhamo could also be effective with Western patients who did not value the diagnosis or treatment. One young Western man in his mid-twenties who was suffering from chronic back pain and stiffness had been persuaded by his friends to see Lhamo. When I spoke to him as he left Lhamo's ritual room, he complained that her diagnosis and her treatment made no sense, and that she had, in fact, hurt him. Lhamo had told him that he had been attacked by a crematorium ghost and by an evil air spirit from behind the stupa. Because the man didn't believe in demonic spirits and he had never been behind the stupa, he thought her diagnosis was off the mark. Lhamo had bit and sucked on his back and had extracted some white stones (white stones, as opposed to black ones, are considered indications that the patient will improve quickly). The man considered the extraction of stones from his body to be a ridiculous sleight of hand.

As he put on his shoes outside Lhamo's apartment, he continued to complain about the diagnosis and about his chronic back pain. He was resistant to the notion of wearing the stones as an amulet, as Lhamo had prescribed. Suddenly, the man stood up and walked around with his hand on his lower back. Looking surprised, he remarked that he felt no pain and that he hadn't felt such freedom of movement in years. He bent down slowly two or three times, as if testing himself. Then, thanking Lhamo's husband and announcing that he would be back, he walked gleefully down the stairs with his friends.

Another male Western patient asked Lhamo to cure his dysentery. However, as she held his hand and felt his pulse with her fingers, she announced that she "saw" that he had a problem with his leg, which he confirmed. Lhamo described it as a numbness and stated that he had been to a doctor and was taking medicine, even before he related his story. The man acknowledged that he had been taking medicine to help alleviate a feeling of numbness that had developed during a trek. He had been worried about the problem for a few weeks, but he hadn't mentioned it because it was on the mend. Both he and the friend who accompanied him were startled by Lhamo's diagnosis, because they had not said anything about the problem beforehand.

The same day, a young American man came in with a sinus headache that Lhamo diagnosed as a case of smoking too much hashish. The young man denied the diagnosis, whereupon Lhamo did another divination, felt his pulse, and repeated the same diagnosis. The man eventually admitted that he had had a drug problem many years ago, but that, for ten years, he had belonged to Narcotics Anonymous and had been drug-free. Then Lhamo told him he also had a heart problem, and she laid him down on the floor and began sucking blood and meat from his chest. Announcing that she needed to restore his heart to its proper position, she pressed a brass mirror containing spiritual healing power against his chest in the four cardinal directions. Then, repeating a mantra, she dusted him with a fan of peacock feathers to brush away the ghosts. When the young man sat up, he confirmed that he had a heart problem but wondered how Lhamo knew about it. A week later, he reported he had been feeling well since Lhamo's healing.

A Frenchman in his mid-thirties spoke to Lhamo about his problems with a girlfriend with whom he'd come to Nepal and who had left him a few days earlier. Lhamo held his hand, felt his pulse, and said something she often tells Westerners: "You think too much." Then she added, "So, you are not married. Before you leave, Lhamo will marry you." Everyone in the room laughed. Then Lhamo, who continued feeling his pulse, interrogated the patient. Her first question, which seemed guided by pure intuition, apparently hit the mark.

"Did you see someone having an accident?" Lhamo asked.

After a long hesitation, the Frenchman answered, "Yes."

"You have been frightened since then?"

"This happened a long time ago."

"Do you think of that accident?"

"Yes."

"Do you dream of that accident?"

"Yes."

"Do you have a heart problem?"

"No."

"Yes," Lhamo countered. "If no girlfriend, you have a heart problem."

Lhamo then sucked on the man's chest and then on his forehead just below the hairline. She spit some blood and meat into a silver bowl that she always uses. Then, examining the extractions with a straw, she said, "Thinking too much! Bad thinking too much! Did you fall on your head?"

"Yes," the man answered.

"Since this, no good thinking." Lhamo advised the Frenchman to return for a fire ceremony. The patient said he would return. After he left, Lhamo stated he had a severe mental problem and that he wouldn't return for the fire ceremony. He didn't.

Although Lhamo often sees almost as many Western patients as she does Nepalese and Tibetan ones, she does not let this go to her head. She treats all who come to see her as equals. She does not hesitate to treat folks who cannot pay, and I have seen her give shelter and food to some who come to see her in desperation. She cares well for her community, and she is respected in turn.

CONCLUSION

Despite the many successful cases described above, it is difficult to estimate Lhamo's overall success rate based on informal observations and anecdotal accounts. Mrs. Dolkar herself estimates her efficacy to be at about seventy-five percent, but her busy schedule makes it difficult to follow up on each case. She may see as many as twenty-five cases each morning. Patients come and go very quickly—most healings last no longer than five minutes. Even in the most difficult and dramatic cases reported above, treatments usually lasted no longer than fifteen to twenty minutes each, and the patients might come for only two or three sessions. The bottom line is that most of her patients clearly believe in her.

Although Lhamo's patients seem content to accept her healing techniques as gifts from the Goddess, as a Western-trained anthropologist and psychotherapist, I often found myself trying to make sense of her shamanic procedures from an empirical perspective. For example, during my initial observations, I became intrigued with trying to discover how Lhamo managed to keep in her mouth all the stuff that she doled out to her patients over a three-hour period. Later, as I began to appreciate the symbolic value and ritual function of these substances, I realized that my preoccupation with identifying their source was immaterial. The important fact was that the extractions seemed to help. Most patients who underwent them reported feeling better, and many commented they felt lighter and more buoyant. After completing each extraction, Lhamo showed the patient the polluted substance and explained its significance, almost as if she were a surgeon who had removed a diseased growth. I could see that, if nothing else, the display of these substances after the extraction served a placebo function, helping Lhamo's patients accept that whatever caused the ailment had been removed, opening the path of healing.

Based on my background in psychology, I interpreted Lhamo's violent exorcisms as psychotherapeutic procedures aimed at breaking down the patient's ego defenses and inducing a psychospiritual crisis. The more her patients express their pain, the more violently she works on them. Then, when they are at their emotional limit, she demands that the evil powers speak through them. Resistance brings more pain.

In one case, Lhamo pulled out a small but impressive amount of hair from a patient's head, lit it on fire, and stuck it in front of the patient, forcing her to deeply inhale the smoke. Lhamo then demanded, "Who are you?" In response, the patient screamed, "*Maasan maasan!*" (an evil ghost). Later Mrs. Dolkar and Pala explained that evil spirits and bokshi are repulsed by the smell of burning hair.

It appears that, by invoking a spirit possession, Lhamo may encourage the communication of important issues—expressed through the voice of the spirit—that need to be worked through. This exorcistic approach allows both the patient's current distress and the previous symptoms and behavior to be blamed on the possessing agent. The patient need not suffer guilt or recrimination for the aberrant behavior caused by the afflicting spirit. Even in cases where the spirit does not communicate understandably—as in the case of the wealthy Nepalese man—the healing process may give the patients or their kin the opportunity to express and come to terms with latent interpersonal issues. Moreover, by bringing problems to the attention of an extended support network during the healing, the patient may receive additional support needed to initiate life changes.

Psychologists Stanislav Grof and Christina Grof (1989, 25) suggest that spirit possession, even in its demonic forms, is potentially a "gateway phenomenon" and that, if the embodying spirit can be encouraged into full emergence, particularly under the protective care of an experienced and fearless healer it can lead to profound transformations

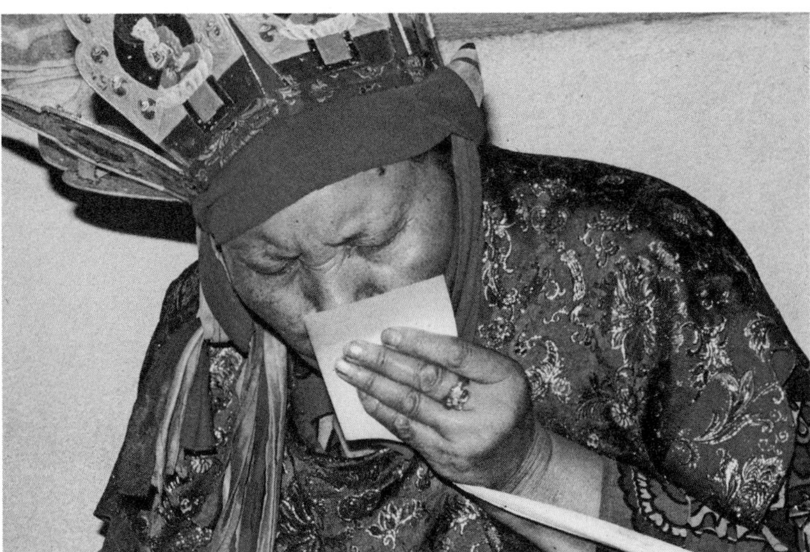

Figure 4-7. Lhamo sometimes performs long-distance healings by sucking on a khata (silk ritual scarf). Photo by Larry Peters

and healings. In many respects, Lhamo's healing exorcisms function as mini-initiations: each patient must undergo a dangerous passage and endure a test of strength and bravery. Not only must patients transcend their pain and confront their demons, but they must also recognize that the fierce attacker before them is a Goddess and an emanation of cosmic compassion.

Despite my insatiable curiosity, I found it impossible to come up with any scientific explanation for some of Lhamo's procedures—such as the long-distance healings she performs using a khatak (long white silk greeting scarf). In this procedure, a person, usually a kin of the absent patient, holds one end of the scarf while Lhamo (sometimes holding a photo of the patient, if one is available) sucks on the other. When she is finished sucking on the khatak, she spits out the patient's illness just as she does for patients who come in person for a healing (see Figure 4-7). Although the mechanism and efficacy of such techniques may continue to defy Western logic, Lhamo's patients are generally not concerned with how they work—only that they do work.

I should point out that Lhamo certainly does not heal everyone, nor is everyone favorably impressed by her methods. There was one woman who came to Lhamo seeking help with a gallstone problem. Lhamo sucked on the woman's belly and produced white stones. She told the patient not to have an operation and that her problem would go away within thirty days. Fortunately, in this case, the woman didn't listen to Lhamo's advice—she decided to go ahead with the operation, and it turned out that it was needed.

One of my colleagues, a professor from the United States, visited me in Nepal with a number of students participating in a semester-abroad program. The students were interested in visiting Lhamo, but they had been warned, by another of my colleagues, that she could be brutal. Apparently Lhamo had hurt her—without healing her. She warned the professor not to take his students to see Lhamo unless they signed liability waivers.

Cautious but curious, the students elected to visit Lhamo, but they all agreed they would not ask for healings. However, on the first visit, Lhamo quickly won them over—perhaps because she showed such care and affection in the case of the young female student described earlier, perhaps because of her astounding accuracy as an oracle, and perhaps because she is a charismatic holy woman. Whatever the cause, many of the students voluntarily stepped forward to Lhamo's altar for healings.

After Lhamo's divination of one student's illness, a nurse in the group declared, for all to hear, "My reality is shattered." There were more shattering revelations that day, as Lhamo proved to be truly psychic with one after another of the students. Many had difficulty watching her intensely aggressive style of healing. From time to time, they would run from the room, only to return in a few moments. By the end of their first visit, most were in awe of her magical abilities and her paranormal knowledge. During the remaining short time they had in Nepal, many of the students flocked to her house to watch her and be with her. Many, like me, became friends of the Dolkars. Later, in follow-up interviews, most said they had learned to "love" and appreciate Mrs. Dolkar's role as Lhamo, and some even had tears in their eyes.

REFERENCES

Berglie, P. A. "Preliminary Remarks on Some Tibetan 'Spirit Mediums' in Nepal." *Kailash: A Journal of Himalayan Research* IV, no. 1 (1976): 85–108.

Dowman, K. *The Great Stupa of Boudhanath,* 2nd ed., revised. Poulnabrucky, Ballyvaughan, Ireland: Footprint Publishing, 1993.

Eliade, M. *Shamanism: Archaic Techniques of Ecstasy.* Translated by W. R. Trask. Princeton, NJ: Bollingen Press, 1964.

Govinda, A. *The Foundation of Tibetan Mysticism.* New York: Samuel Weiser, 1969.

Grof, S., and C. Grof. *Spiritual Emergency: When Personal Transformation Becomes a Crisis.* Los Angeles: Jeremy Tarcher, 1989.

Harner, M. *The Way of the Shaman,* 10th anniversary edition. San Francisco: Harper & Row Publishers, 1990.

Holmberg, D. *Order in Paradox: Myth, Ritual, and Exchange among Nepal's Tamang.* Ithaca, NY: Cornell University Press, 1989.

Ingerman, S. *Soul Retrieval.* San Francisco: Harper & Row Publishers, 1991.

Lewis, I. M. *Ecstatic Religion: A Study of Shamanism and Spirit Possession,* 2nd ed. New York: Routledge & Kegan Paul, 1989.

Mumford, S. R. *Himalayan Dialogues: Tibetan Lamas and Gurung Shamans in Nepal.* Madison: University of Wisconsin Press, 1989.

Nebesky-Wojkowitz, R. de. *Oracles and Demons of Tibet: The Cult and Iconography of the Tibetan Protective Deities.* Kathmandu: Tiwari's Pilgrims Book House, 1993.

Norbu, N. *Drung, Deu and Bön: Narrations, Symbolic Languages and the Bön Tradition in Ancient Tibet.* Translated by A. Clemente and A. Lukianowica. Dharamsala, India: Library of Tibetan Works and Archives, 1995.

Peters, L. *Ecstasy and Healing in Nepal.* Malibu, CA: Undena Press, 1981.

Peters, L., and D. Price-Williams. "Towards an Experiential Analysis of Shamanism." *American Ethnologist* 7, no. 3 (1980): 397–418.

Sagant, P. *The Dozing Shaman: The Limbus of Eastern Nepal.* Translated by N. Scott. Oxford: Oxford University Press, 1996.

Samuel, G. *Civilized Shamans: Buddhism in Tibetan Studies.* Washington, DC: Smithsonian Institution Press, 1993.

Shirokogoroff, S. M. *Psychomental Complex of the Tungus.* London: Routledge & Kegan Paul, Ltd., 1935.

·5·

THE *YETI*

Spirit of Himalayan Forest Shamans

> Ban jhankri *or "forest wizards" are an almost unknown forest tribe credited with great powers of healing.*
>
> M. P. Koirala, Former Prime Minister of Nepal (quoted in Coleman 1989, 35)

The yeti is widely known but not well understood. Its physical presence, accepted as fact by most Himalayan people, was the subject of much scientific study. In the end, reports and evidence of its physical existence failed to meet the scrutiny of paleontology and zoology. But the yeti has a ubiquitous presence in Himalayan culture. It is a living, current, popular mythology and a folkloric treasure whose origins I seek to uncover in this chapter. Yeti were originally fierce spirits of nature—mountain goddesses and forest wildmen of the pre-Buddhist Bönpo shamanism of Tibet. They are principal characters in a vast oral mythology of becoming a shaman. A spiritual biography of the yeti is described from the perspective of an anthropology of consciousness and history of Tibetan religions.

THE *YETI* AND THE *BAN JHANKRI*

The *ban jhankri* (male forest shaman) of the Nepal Himalayas, and his spouse, the *ban jhankrini,* are thought to be spirits or deities who initiate shamans, as well as living creatures with a partially human physical presence. The males are half-monkey, half-human guru of shamans. Ban jhankri is also the Nepali name for a specific type of yeti described as being three to five feet tall and, except for face and hands, covered from head to toe with thick red or golden hair. Nepalese shamans say his wife, the ban jhankrini, is a much more formidable mixture of human and simian or bear standing twelve to fifteen feet tall with thick, long black hair. These two types of yeti are the mythical and spiritual progenitors of many forms of Nepalese and Tibetan shamanism.

All types of yeti, including ban jhankri, are indigenously believed to be living vestiges of the ancient past. At the same time, the yeti and the ban jhankri are characters in a vast oral mythology, one that is not merely a story told but a reality lived in culture, consciousness, and the initiations of Nepalese shamans. It is a current, living mythology, not a fossil but a recognized way to become a shaman.

According to legend and personal reports of shamans who have encountered them, the ban jhankri kidnap potential shamans, typically between seven and seventeen years of age, and bring them into the forests and caves where they live in order to teach and initiate them. During abduction, the ban jhankri causes his candidates to become naked so he may inspect them for spiritual imperfections. Only candidates who are pure (*chokho*) in body and heart-mind (*man*[41]) are accepted for teaching, most often for a few days up to a week but sometimes for a month, a year, or even more before being returned, often to the place of their abduction. Candidates who do not pass inspection because they are spiritually impure (jutho) are "thrown" from the cave by the ban jhankri or worse, by his big, ferocious wife, who threatens to "kill" her husband's novices to "cut off" their limbs and heads with her golden blade, and to "eat" them.

The purpose of this chapter is to point to an often-neglected identity in the anthropology of the Himalaya, between the two genders of yeti and the two genders of ban jhankri (or forest shaman), by discussing their parallel, analogous, and often-identical legends, encounters with humans, nomenclature, and their physical resemblance described in folklore. The method utilized attempts to integrate the personal stories I've collected from Nepalese ban jhankri shaman initiate abductees with the ethnographies of other researchers to demonstrate the relevance of the yeti legend to this highly prevalent Himalayan shamanic experience.

THE MYTHIC CONTEXT OF *YETI* RESEARCH

The yeti is mythologically categorized as a type of "Bigfoot" with analogies in many parts of the world (Napier 1973, 34). Specifically, however, when one thinks of the yeti, one thinks of a tall, burly, long-haired, elusive, intelligent ape-man inhabiting the snowcapped Tibet-Nepal Himalaya. The yeti is well regarded in Nepal, Tibet, and other Himalayan cultures, and the subject of a large body of folklore. The government airline, Royal Nepal Airlines, boasts of offering "Yeti Service," and a tall, big-footed, ape-like yeti statue carrying a tray of drinks adorns the grounds in front of its Kathmandu headquarters (see Figure 5-1). A yeti likeness has been on display in the Kathmandu Museum of Natural History, and one is featured on a Bhutanese postage stamp. Commercial products, magazines, hotels, restaurants, companies, and shops are named after it.

Expeditions have been launched to sight yeti. *World Book Encyclopedia* sponsored one by Sir Edmund Hillary, who was joined by noted American zoologist Marlin Perkins (Hillary and Doig 1962). Millionaire oilman and explorer Tom Slick led three expeditions; and numerous adventurers, mountain climbers, and scientists made equally sincere attempts. Because yeti have fascinated Western curiosity, novels have been written, and fictional and documentary films produced (see Chorvinsky 1989, 135–149). There was so much interest in the yeti that, in 1958, the Nepalese government, recognizing its value as

Figure 5-1. Statue of a yeti outside the main office of Nepal Airlines in Kathmandu.
Photo by Larry Peters.

a source of national revenue, declared the yeti a protected species, and made it illegal to hunt or try to capture one without a special license costing the handsome sum of £400 (Napier 1973, 47, 48).

Yeti scalps, fur skins, skeletal hands, and other yeti "relics" that are sacred to the Sherpa are kept in protected cases at Buddhist monasteries in the Everest region. Unusual five-toed plantigrade footprints purported to belong to yeti have been found, cast, and photographed, generally described with the large toe splayed out, facing backward, and nonopposable to the other toes. From the evidence of the footprints, two types of yeti have been identified: a large yeti with footprints approximately twelve inches long and eight inches wide (approximately three times the width of the average human foot) and a stride nearly twice that of a human, and a small yeti with a footprint roughly half that size (Napier 1973, 53). The larger creature was hypothesized to be a living representative of *Gigantopithecus,* an anthropoid or perhaps early hominid of the mid-Pleistocene whose fossil record suggests that some had resided in the Himalayan foothills, possibly coexisting with *Homo erectus* in parts of Southeast Asia, and became extinct about five hundred thousand years ago (Gupta and Nath 1994, 111–119; Lall 1988a, 18; Napier 1973, 23; Strasenburgh 1999, 551). The smaller was most often identified as Neanderthal (Napier 1973, 181–190; Shackley 1983, 98). Less frequently, yeti were categorized as *Australopithecus* (Panday 1994, 42). The smaller and larger varieties of yeti identified by the Western researchers corresponded with the folkloric notions of the Sherpa: the *dzu-te* (*dzu* = livestock), a large creature that preys on cattle, and the small *me-te* (*me* = man, *te* = bear) said to be as small as a "fourteen-year-old boy" but stout like a man with thick shoulders, and monkey-like, with red hair covering his body (Coleman 1989, 43; Napier 1973, 58; Panday 1994, 52; Sanderson 1961, 268–270). Me-te is discussed below.

Nearly all of this "data," however, has been determined to be scientifically suspect. The scalps examined were not even primates', but serows'. Most footprints could be attributed to bear; some of the fur skins, like the scalps, were serows', and others were bears'; one skeletal "hand" belonged to a snow leopard and another was part-monkey/part-human wired together. The distinguished anthropologist John Napier (1973, 18), writing about the material evidence for the existence of the yeti, says, "... fragments of 'evidence' such as scalps, mummified hands, droppings, scraps of hair, and so on have been produced from time to time but, without exception, all have been shown to be either fakes or irrelevancies. The only form of material evidence available to us is footprints and, at best, they have only a circumstantial value."

The yeti remains kept by the Sherpa are jealously guarded sacred objects. Even so, the lama allowed some of the explorers to briefly examine and photograph them. Scientific analyses of these were, of course, inconclusive. Thus physical evidence was needed for an examination under laboratory conditions. Almost all the explorers and yeti researchers respected the Sherpas' reverence for the yeti bones. However, on one occasion, overzealous Western investigators absconded with fragments of the yeti hand at Pangboche monastery, secretly replacing them with a human *sacra*. The scientific analysis was never completed, and the location of these yeti bones is not currently known (Coleman 1989, 90–92).

All the expeditionary efforts to sight a yeti fell short. In the end only Sherpa and other indigenes claimed to have been close enough to identify a yeti with convincing certainty (Lall 1988a, 69–70). A few Westerners claimed to have seen one from long distances but were unable to follow it. A humorous Sherpa anecdote suggests that, because the yeti's feet face backward (heel forward), as told in the folktales, Westerners who have attempted to track them have inevitably gone in the opposite direction. Commenting on the fact that Westerners never see yeti, the abbot of Tyangboche monastery said, "While you *sahibs* are about, they never appear" (Lall 1988a, 3). One reason suggested, according to "modern" Nepalese folklore, is that the smell of gunpowder carried by Westerners on their expeditions is repugnant to the yeti (Lall 1988a, 39–40). They are also afraid of fire (Nebesky-Wojkowitz 1956, 159).

It is believed that yeti encounters only happen by chance. The Sherpas say, "If you look for him you will never find him" (Messner 2000, 142). However, there are various seemingly fantastic accounts told by Westerners that are difficult to accept as evidence for yeti, but that may be part of larger, worldwide, archetypal "wildman" and "monster" mythologies, elements of which are shared in common with the yeti stories of the Himalayan people (cf. Napier 1973, 24, 31). For example, there is the story told by an injured climber who said he was rescued in the Himalaya by a giant, hairy yeti who, as it turned out, was a member of a lost prehistoric tribe; she took him to her cave, nursed him for weeks to complete recovery, and returned him to civilization (see Napier 1973, 41). Reinhold Messner, acknowledged as one of the world's greatest mountain climbers, and a serious student of the yeti, had a "yeti encounter" while trekking alone in Tibet in 1986 that deeply affected his life. In his book *My Quest for the Yeti* (2000), he came to believe that the yeti he encountered was a species of bear (*Ursus arctos*) and that this was the same species around which Sherpa and other Tibetans had developed their yeti legend (Messner 2000, 147). Many bear/yeti identity theories have been advanced (see Napier 1973, 147–153).

There are no photographs of the yeti (Panday 1994, 26). Even so, the yeti created a sensation when it was first reported in the West, at the turn of the last century, as well as throughout its "golden age" of popularity in the 1950s until the late 1960s (Napier 1973, 47).

Most Himalayan people assume the existence of the yeti. Milarepa, the highly respected twelfth-century Tibetan Buddhist hermit, poet, saint, and *yogi,* mentions encountering a demon commonly thought to be a yeti (Lall 1988a, 23, 25; Panday 1994, 36, 51). An eighteenth-century Tibetan medical text describes a half-man, half-ape creature covered with long hair that is thought to be a yeti (Lall 1988a, 23–24). The Himalayan people believe yeti were much more plentiful and have become rare due to human aggression (Lall 1988b, 18–19). However, even today, stories about the yeti are integral to the culture. Most see yeti folklore as history, and it seems nearly everyone has a story to tell about someone who has encountered one. The yeti is a common focal point of conversation among the Sherpa (Hagen 1961, 75). Although only a few first-person encounters by indigenes have been recorded by anthropologists and folklorists (Napier 1973, 63), the firm belief in the yeti by the majority of the people is what likely helped convince Westerners to embark on numerous expeditions to find one.

In 1960, Khunjo Chumbi, a Sherpa, along with Sir Edmund Hillary, received permission from the Sherpa community to bring a reputedly 240-year-old sacred "yeti scalp," worn in sacred dances at

Khumjung monastery, to Europe for examination. Even when confronted with scientific conclusions as to the scalp's lack of authenticity, Chumbi was reported to have said, "In Nepal, we have neither giraffe nor kangaroo. Hence, most people know nothing about these animals. In France, there are no yeti, so I sympathize with your ignorance" (Panday 1994, 83). Similarly, Desmond Doig, the Sherpa who accompanied Hillary's failed yeti expedition and coauthored the book in which Hillary debunks the yeti and writes its epitaph, continued to defend the yeti's existence (Lall 1988a, 5).

Lall (1988a, 60–70) believes that, if it wasn't for the Sherpa, there would not be yeti, as the yeti is their folkloric gift to the world. They are the ones who identified the first strange footprints found in the high snows as yeti to Western climbers and vouched for the authenticity of the yeti "relics." Western explorers mention that nearly every unexplainable footprint that is not directly attributable to some animal is likely to be identified as yeti (Napier 1973, 224). Such is an indication of the ubiquity of the yeti in the mind of the folk.

In many Tibetan and Sherpa folktales, the yeti is portrayed as an existent, biological, cultural, and intellectual predecessor of humanity. The history of mankind is conceived as passing through stages of development (Stein 1972, 45). In Sherpa art on the monastery walls and when portrayed on thangka (painted scrolls) used for meditation, the yeti appear higher than animals and below humans (Messner 2000, 76). In broad outline, this mythic model corresponded to the spirit of the evolutionism of many Western investigators and undoubtedly contributed to a mutual validation of belief, and fostered a partnership between natives and researchers over the years, in a quest to find the "missing link" yeti and empirically prove its existence to the world.

These evolutionary views, which are characteristic of ancient, pre-Buddhist Tibetan culture, changed over time as the Tibetans assimilated the Hindu-Buddhist philosophy of the progressive degeneration of humankind from a sacred "Golden Era" or "Truth Era"

(Stein 1972, 45). Regarding the yeti, the people hold both views simultaneously, even though they are contradictory. The yeti is an ape and partially human but, at the same time (as will be discussed later), is a demigod of the pristine Golden times.

Much of the scientific research on the yeti has been concerned with it as a physical animal within the hierarchy of nature. However, there is another area of research too, the cultural, which is concerned with how people think and therefore the myths and legends that reveal the character and personality of the yeti and its spiritual role in Himalayan culture.

YETI CULTURE AND PERSONALITY IN LEGEND

The etymology of the term yeti is not definite, nor clear. It has varied interpretations, and a review of these may prove to have heuristic value in providing background information regarding the beliefs about the origins and character of the yeti. The term yeti is not universally known in Tibet. Norbu (Norbu and Turnbull 1972, 69), abbot of the Kumbum monastery in Tibet until 1949, had never heard the term referred to in Tibet and believes it is a Nepalese term. In Tibetan, *yeh* (or *ye*) may refer to "rocky places" (see Coleman 1989, 43). According to most philologists, yeti is derived from *me-te* (*me* = man; *te* = bear), the brown bear (colloquially "red bear") so called because it often walks on its hind feet like a man, thus "bear-man" (see Majupuria and Kumar 1993, 46; Pravananda 1955, 99–101; cf. Sanderson 1961, 268–269). Dre (*de*), another popular term, is a small demon (e.g., goblin, imp, or gnome) and an evil spirit (Jäschke 1972, 284). There is another linguistic analysis that dismisses the *te* = bear hypothesis and instead posits that *te* (*tse* in written Tibetan) means "life" or "living thing." Thus *me-te* means "man-like living thing that is not a human being" nor is it a bear (Aharon 1961, 460–462; see Napier 1973, 58). Aharon (1961, 457–458, 460, 462) maintains yeti is a Tibetan loan-word adopted into Nepalese, and suggests that there is a meaningful "connection" between the Tibetan term yeti and the Nepalese third-person pronouns *yi* (these) and *ti* (those, implying at a distance), which yields a Tibetan-Nepali semantic compound that can be translated in informal speech as "that there thing." Another name mentioned often, *me-te* (or *toh*) *kangme* (snowman), could mean man-like living snow-thing or snow-bear, mistranslated in 1921 by Henry Newman, the journalist-explorer, as the "abominable snowman" (Majupuria and Kumar 1993, 46). Sherpas often use the term *ya* (or *yeh*)*-te,* connoting a cliff-dwelling thing/bear of the high regions (Majupuria and Kumar 1993, 5; Panday 1994, i, 19). Pravananda (1955, 100–102), the Indian philologist, offers another perspective, which I believe deserves more attention. He says *yeh-ti* (*yeti*) was originally a mythical all-devouring rocky-place or mountain demon whose name was later applied to the "snowman" as a pejorative epithet. So, just as we might call a particularly savage and voracious beast "monster," the ancient Tibetans called it yeti (see Coleman 1989, 44).[42]

The most common folktale of the origin of the yeti tells of a young Tibetan girl who was lost in the forest, then abducted by and mated with a large ape, from which issued the half-ape, half-human yeti. However, there is another widely known story that, in my opinion, is a better candidate and a more fully developed myth for the origin of the yeti. This story is the Tibetan anthropogeny, as well as the story of the creation of culture. It tells that Tibetan people descended from a cannibalistic rock ogress (a sin-mo) and a monkey. From their union issued six male children who were half-human and half-ape. They stood erect, were covered with long hair, and had flat, red faces and tails. The parents set aside a forested area in the Yarlung Valley in central Tibet for their children. Here the six brothers mated with monkeys, giving rise to the six "earliest tribes" from which Tibetans claim ancestry (Stein 1972, 28, 37, 46). These half-ape progenitors of humankind are called "wild people," just as the yeti are (Stein 1972, 28). Further, they are described as "little men" or "dwarfs" (Stein 1972, 46). Such descriptions of long-haired forest men, wildmen, little men, ape-men, and male protohuman forebearers are characteristic of the ban jhankri or small type of yeti. Perhaps the big, cannibalistic rock demoness is an early representation of the larger type of yeti; that is, the sin-mo demoness from which the epithet yeti was derived? Sin-mo (or srin-mo) are a class of fierce mountain goddesses of the pre-Buddhist Bön faith of Tibet (Nebesky-Wojkowitz 1993, 280–281).

Both the ogress sin-mo and the monkey were later assimilated into Buddhist lore as deities. In the process, the monkey was seen to be an emanation of Chenrezig, the patron deity of Tibet, and the sin-mo as an emanation of Tara, his likewise compassionate consort (Samuel 1993, 168, 222, 483; Stein 1972, 28, 46). In other words, they were converted from Bön to Buddhist deities. In other versions of the same story, the ape first converts to Buddhism and then mates with the rock demoness (Ekvall 1964, 87–88). This is the same as the Everest region Sherpa version collected by Messner (2000, 77–78). In this version, the rock demoness remains a demonic nonconvert to Buddhism.

It is believed that the ogress and the monkey bequeathed to the Tibetan people the contrasting parts that constitute their character. From the monkey emanation of the father, they inherited some traits of Chenrezig: the "civilizing" Buddhist virtues of compassion, hard-working diligence, and a religious nature. From their mother, they received their pre-Buddhist "wild" and "untamed" propensities: quick temper, passionate nature, proneness to jealousy, and fondness for play and meat (Samuel 1993, 168, 222).

The characters embodied in the pre-Buddhist versions of the story fall into two general folklore categories: i.e., that of "monsters" who are big, ugly, and dangerous; and "wildmen" who are smaller, ape-like, more humanoid, and of the forests rather than the high mountains (Napier 1973, 22–23; Sanderson 1961, 268–272). The Himalayan yeti of folklore is of both types, and the big monster is always related in some way to the wildman, either as spouse or sibling. Further and more importantly, they are characters in the same story with interdependent roles. As will be shown later, they are inseparable ingredients in the oral mythos for becoming a shaman.

According to the Sherpa, one of the yeti's traditional abodes is the Mahalangur Himalayan range, or Great Monkey Mountains, which are located in the vicinity of Everest and Makalu. As no species of monkey are said to exist in the area, and Mahalangur is a Nepali appellation given to the yeti, this range in northeastern Nepal was often chosen as a favorite place for expeditions (Coleman 1989, 45; Majupuria and Kumar 1993, 5; Panday 1994, 1–2). However, yeti are believed to exist throughout the Himalayan regions, in central and southern Nepal, as well as in India. Indeed, some scholars believe yeti is thematically and linguistically related to *yaksa* (Sanskrit), a wild, intelligent, dwarf-like, half-human, half-animal Hindu and Buddhist demigod, covered with long hair, credited with the power to appear and disappear instantaneously, who, it is said, frequents caves and other isolated and solitary places inhabited by yogi (Gupta and Nath 1994, 63–64; Nebesky-Wojkowitz 1993, 42). On the other hand, the *yakshini* or *yaksi,* their female counterparts, are ancient, fierce Mother Goddesses akin to Kali, Durga, and especially Harati, the "Mother of Demons," a "chief witch" and "stealer of children" (Eliade 1958, 345–346; Schuhmacher and Woerner 1989, 422; Waddell 1971, 369). Yakshini are reputed to cannibalize children (Basham 1954, 317; Dietrich 1998, 60; O'Flaherty 1976, 78), and kidnappings by the yakshini may be part of a novice East Indian shaman's Kali initiation (Bhairavan 2000, xvii, 14). Thus yeti and/or yeti analogues are found over a large geographic area of South Asia from the Indian plains to the Himalaya of Nepal, Tibet, and adjacent regions, with linguistic cognates attributed to two distinct language families (Tibeto-Burmese and Indo-European). By whatever regional name she or he is known, yeti is a prominent legendary character in many of the diverse cultural groups (Indian and Tibetan) who speak these languages.

Three types of yeti are frequently identified in Tibetan and Nepali folklore and legend. The first is called *nyalmo* in Tibetan (Gupta and Nath 1994, 46, 100, 101; Majupuria and Kumar 1993, 12–13; Panday 1994, 36, 52). It is huge (twelve to fifteen feet tall), powerful, dangerous, and carnivorous. It is thought these large yeti are ape- or bear-like, half-human, but with a protruding jaw that is sometimes described as a long snout like that of a wolf. The yogi and Nepalese anthropologist Narahari Nath described his sighting of a yeti, possibly of this type, as a giant over twelve feet tall, with long, dangling arms and a thick coat of black and gray hair, who walked with long strides and had extraordinary strength and endurance. In 1968, Nath sighted this yeti while on pilgrimage to Mt. Kailash in Tibet, when it carried off one of his large yak pack animals. He unsuccessfully attempted to photograph it. His Sherpa guide was overcome with fear and fainted at the sight, but believed their lives were spared because Nath wore the robes of a follower of Shiva, whom the yeti revere. Nath made numerous Himalayan pilgrimages, but this was his only yeti sighting (Gupta and Nath 1994, 29, 61–63).

Nyalmo yeti (like the dzu-te) are said to prey on yak, cattle, and other large animals, and are reputed to be man-eaters with a fondness for human brain. According to folklore, nyalmo are female and matriarchal, and are said to mate with their human male captives (Dhakal 1991, 88–91; Gupta and Nath 1994, 100–101; Panday 1994, 8–10, 17–18, 28). They live in the highest tracts of the mountain forest, and the Sherpa believe these are the beings who leave large tracks in the snow while ostensibly foraging for food (Nebesky-Wojkowitz 1956, 160; 1993, 344 n. 1).

According to popular folklore, these female nyalmo yeti have large, sagging breasts that hang down well below their waists that they sling over their nape when they rest and carry in their hands when they run downhill. Lore suggests the best way to escape from these yeti is to run downhill. Their hair blocks their vision, and their long breasts need to be held in both hands to prevent stumbling over them. When running uphill, their breasts are slung over their napes, enabling them to be much faster (Coleman 1989, 34; Majupuria and Kumar 1993, 30; Panday 1994, iv).

Both male and female yeti are amorous; there are many reports of mating with humans, and mixed yeti/human families (Dhakal 1991, 70–76, 88–91; Gupta and Nath 1994, 76–87). Ganesh Bajra Lama, a Tamang lama of Boudhanath, my main ethnographic field site, told me about a family comprised of a female yeti and male Sherpa from the Helambu region. They and their children are very tall, hairy, burly-gorilla appearing, and wild in nature, and live apart from the villagers and near the forest. They are known in the area as the "nyalmo family."

The female is thought to be both highly sexual and rageful (Panday 1994, 18). In one popular story, a female yeti bears a child fathered by a captured human whom she had forced to be a reproductive slave. He escapes and she, knowing he loves the child, waits for him to turn around so he can see her brutally kill the child by smashing its head with a rock, and then eats its brain (Lall 1988a, 29–31).

From all these descriptions, the nyalmo yeti is a semihuman, fierce, sexually aggressive mountain demoness, probably not unlike the cannibalistic rock ogress (sin-mo) in the Tibetan descent-of-man story. In a Buddhist version of the story, the rock-mountain ogress "forced" the monkey emanation of the patron deity out of his meditation and celibate purity to father the wildmen ancestors of the Tibetan people (Samuel 1993, 222).

Nyalpa (*ba*) is Tibetan for coitus. *Nyalbu* is the bastard child of a whore. *Mo* is the usual suffix indicating female gender. Nyalmo is thus a lascivious female beast. The term also can refer to filth and foul things (Das 1974, 478; Jäschke 1972, 186). In myth, yeti lairs and bodies are said to reek of garlic and thus be spiritually impure (see Chophel 1993, 22). If the meanings of nyalmo and yeti are compounded, it leaves one with the striking image of an unbridled, rapacious, lustful, wild, cannibalistic, terrifying, kidnapping, dark, huge, hairy, bear/ape/human-like, foul-smelling, spiritually polluted, murderous demoness roaming the Himalaya. Like the Tamang, Bhote (people of Tibetan descent) currently living in the Hinduized Kathmandu Valley say nyalmo are forest Kali (*ban kali*), fierce deities of the hunt. It is thought that these fierce goddesses have, at their command, a host of demons and spirits, including the potentially helpful but often dangerous *sikhari* or hunter spirits.

Children are especially frightened, as the big yeti is a sort of bogeyman utilized by parents as a threat: "Don't do … or the yeti will take you" (Majupuria and Kumar 1993, 10; Panday 1994, 44). Indeed, there are numerous stories of children being kidnapped by yeti. In some of these reports, the yeti feed and care for the needs of their young captives. However, the female is covetous and, if she catches anyone trying to escape, they are killed and cannibalized. If they escape, they return home naked and behaving wildly, having forgotten cultural norms. It can take years to readjust to social life after the trauma (Gupta and Nath 1994, 65–67, 101). Big yeti are frightening to adults as well, as the mere sight of one can cause ague, madness, coma, or even death (Choden 1997, 85, 130; Panday 1994, 32). Explorers report that, after finding a large footprint in the snow and hearing a loud, unexplained noise, if their guides and porters were convinced it was yeti, they became panic-stricken and, in some cases, dropped their loads and ran off, leaving their Western charges alone (Coleman 1989, 34).

Yet, big yeti often have an instructive relationship with anchorite yogi, whose powers of concentration, purpose, and compassion they test by their frightening appearance. Yeti bestow spiritual insights on the wise men they encounter who succeed in conquering their fear (Choden 1997, 53). To those of guileless disposition, they gift power objects, like "magic wands," to help overcome adversity (Sharma 1996, 87–91). In some stories, the yeti is a form taken by a deity to challenge the yogi and ultimately guide him toward liberation (Choden 1997, 73). Yeti appear only to those whom they deem to be worthy due to their noble human qualities (Choden 1997, 53) or righteousness (Messner 2000, 35) and predestined ability to communicate with spirits and demons (Choden 1997, xii–xiii, 137). Yogi of the Himalayan caves say that fierce mountain deities like the yeti reveal their teachings only to the "pure in heart" (Evans-Wentz 1951, 17).

In one Buddhist folktale, a yeti offered Buddha fruit to aid his meditation; for doing this, Buddha bestowed supernatural powers on the yeti (Wangdi 1994, 3). Thus yeti are sacred as well as polluted. They are respected as sacred beings (Gupta and Nath 1994, 100). They are revered for their spiritual powers but, at the same time, rageful demons that are feared and dangerous.

Buddhism in Tibet and among the Sherpa is a history of the conquering and conversion of the old Bönpo (shamanic)[43] mountain gods and goddesses, many of whom were not unlike the nyalmo yeti, by such Buddhist hero saints as Padma Sambhava (Guru Rinpoche) and Milarepa (Chang 1962, Part One; Paul 1982, 76–80; Samuel 1993, 168). In the process, which Samuel (1993, 217–220) sees as part of a large-scale cultural "taming" from nomadism to agriculturalism, Bönpo shamanism to Buddhism, many of the old mountain deities were subsumed into Tibetan Buddhism and, while retaining their original fierceness, became demigod protectors (Sanskrit: dharmapala) who aid in the defeat of all human and supernatural foes of Buddhism (Nebesky-Wojkowitz 1993, 3). Thus, "enemies" of the Buddhist faith in the Tibetan anthropogeny discussed above were remade into its protectors. The yeti, however, remained elusive. The sin-mo, while eventually identified with the Buddhist Tara in some versions, remained a nonconvert in others. In the latter, she is not a Buddhist protector but rather a pre-Buddhist progenitor of "wild people." She herself is uncontained, sexual, murderous, and cannibalistic and, according to the Tibetans themselves, has bequeathed a host of inherited personality traits that contradict Buddhist ideals. That is to say, she has not been incorporated into Buddhism in any substantial way, any more than into paleontology or zoology. These yeti are popular, and are highly present in folktales and in the imagination of the indigenous people of the Himalaya, but their spiritual significance is buried deep in the pre-Buddhist antiquity of shamanism.

The second type of yeti is typically the *ri mi,* less frequently the *chut-te* (Tibetan and Sherpa). The latter is a bipedal omnivore whose size varies in description, from that of a rhesus monkey, to that of a human adult (five to six feet tall), to that of the nyalmo. It lives in the forest and caves at altitudes between eight and ten thousand feet, below the habitat of the nyalmo. They are reputed to often stay near streams and lakes, where they enjoy consuming the local species of frogs. Consequently, these yeti are known as "water yeti" (Majupuria and Kumar 1993, 13–14; Panday 1994, 41). Ri mi or mountain men are about eight feet tall. They are hairy, midsize yeti with thick necks (Gupta and Nath 1994, 46, 101; Lall 1988a, 25). Unfortunately, not much else is known about chut-te and ri mi.

The smallest and swiftest yeti is called ban jhankri or *rang shi bompo* (Tibetan: self-generated shaman; *bombo* in Tamang)[44] and is described by Helambu Sherpa and Tamang as a spontaneously appearing and disappearing being whose presence is sudden, unexpected, and self-determined. Bombo means shaman, as does jhankri, and, like shamans, these yeti are also thought to have mystical powers (Gupta and Nath 1994, 84; Lall 1988a, 24). Rang shi bombo (or ban jhankri), like the Sherpa me-te, stand three to five feet tall. For this reason, some Western explorers have called them "minor yeti" (Gupta and Nath 1994, 29). They have reddish, white, or golden hair covering their bodies, short legs, and wrinkled faces like orangutan. Sen Tenzing, a Sherpa who was on the 1951 Everest expedition of the mountain climber Eric Shipton, described sighting a yeti seemingly of this type, half-human/half-beast, standing five and a half feet tall with a pointed head and body covered with reddish-brown hair but with a hairless face (Coleman 1989, 40; Sanderson 1961, 270; Saunders 1995, 144).

It is believed this type was previously found in large numbers in the Helambu region. Ganesh Bajra Lama, the Tamang lama from Boudhanath mentioned above, in his youth made expeditions in this area to find them, and reports locating their caves about forty years ago. He says their nests are made of juniper, moss, and grass, and they have neither fire nor crafted weapons. This is also maintained in numerous folktales. However, it is believed they use rocks as weapons. There are many more native sightings of this type. Some Western explorers came to believe that the yeti was less of a snowman than a forest man and shifted their focus to the lower altitudes. They did not find any, but believed there was ample evidence (e.g., footprints) to suggest the existence of a small, intelligent, inquisitive, ape-like animal dwelling in the Himalayan forests of Nepal (Coleman 1989, 76–77; Gupta and Nath 1994, 101–102).

According to legend, this group of yeti, unlike nyalmo, is patriarchal and male. They are amorous toward their human female captives. Most believe these yeti live in the forests and caves at altitudes below the snow line and are mostly vegetarian. They are sometimes reported coming into villages to steal grain, flour, and milk. In Tibetan, "playing yeti" has the connotation of "to rob" (Messner 2000, 76). Rang shi bombo walk upright. They can be dangerous and will attack, but only if provoked (Lall 1988a, 39–48).

Despite differences in the folklore of height, color, and resemblance to different animals, both genders of yeti have many traits in common. They are partially human in appearance. Their heads are conical or egg-shaped. All yeti have long hair, long arms, thick shoulders, short necks, relatively short legs, and feet that point backward. They are bipedal except when climbing. They sometimes eat with the backs of their hands. They are nocturnal with keen eyesight at night. They have long ears and correspondingly acute hearing. In some folktales, they have human speech; in others, they are thought to roar like a tiger, yelp, bleat, make a "koo koo" sound, or emit a high-pitched whistle. Some use telepathy and thought projection to communicate their notions to humans. They are reputed to live more than three hundred years. Their spirit can be invoked from their bones (Lall 1988b, 23), which also provide protection from sorcerers (Macdonald 1976, 339 n. 67). Their blood is thought to give magical potency to objects with which it comes into contact (Choden 1997, 42) and is used in the preparation of healing remedies (Nebesky-Wojkowitz 1956, 158). Their gall is a cure for jaundice, and their meat a cure for mental diseases (Lall 1988a, 24) and, when used as a ritual offering, it will pacify wrathful spirits and gain their aid (Nebesky-Wojkowitz 1993, 343–344).

Yeti are said to possess the entire gamut of human emotions, ranging from ferocity to love for spouses, friends, and children. They cry when their feelings are hurt, and there are legends about yeti who committed suicide out of despair. They may beg for mercy to save their children's lives. Another story tells about a yeti that saved a human life (Gupta and Nath 1994, 81).

Yeti are prone to uncritical thinking and imitative behaviors that clever humans have used to trick and thereby escape from them, capture them, or even kill them. They have a fondness for alcohol that has likewise contributed to their declining population (Chophel 1984, 76, 115; Lall 1988b, 14). Generally, they are thought to be wild, half-animal, and unaware of human propensities toward subterfuge and aggression.

On the other hand, yeti are thought to have shamanic abilities like ESP. They are able to "see" and "hear" over long distances (Gupta and Nath 1994, 84). They do divination by inspecting the body parts of recently killed animals, just as human shamans do (Lall 1988a, 34). They have been sighted doing community rituals after a hunting kill and during the full moon (Gupta and Nath 1994, 100). They have the ability to shape-shift into almost any animal (Lall 1988a, 48) and to become invisible, i.e., to appear and disappear instantly, manifesting in tangible form and then vanishing (Choden 1997, 37; Gupta and Nath 1994, 84; Messner 2000, 18; Panday 1994, iv).

BAN JHANKRI[45]

Generally speaking, the Tamang and Magar with whom I have conducted ethnographic research recognize that there are two major types of yeti and that these two kinds of yeti correspond to the two types of ban jhankri: the large female and the small male. Most are also aware that some of the names that identify yeti also identify ban jhankri. The ferocious mate of the ban jhankri is often called nyalmo, just like the big yeti; and the small yeti is named ban jhankri. Still, their identity is not generally acknowledged by the lay folk. When people think of yeti, the image that seems to be conjured up is that of the frightening large bear-like or ape-like creature whose identity as an ancient mountain goddess and connection to shamanism or any type of spirituality are all but lost. When people think of the ban jhankri, they think of the creature that initiates shamans. The small yeti is seen as a wild forest man, a thief of grain, milk, and other farm products, somewhat of a nuisance. Focusing on these disparate characteristics keeps them separate in the mind of the people; therefore, the ban jhankri and small yeti are distinct to some.

When I would press this issue in conversation, and remind people of their identical names and physical appearance, and congruence in some legends, the answer was, more often than not, "Yes, why not?," acknowledging that I was surely right but they hadn't thought about it before. This type of answer was less than satisfying, and such ethnographic data was contrary to the ideas coalescent in my thinking. Nevertheless, it is the case that yeti folklore has become a widespread cultural phenomenon that has reached international proportions and has developed well beyond its epithetic origins, whereas the ban jhankri is the limited concern of Himalayan shamans. There are no mountain travel agents nor mountain airlines named after the ban jhankri, nor do Kathmandu vendors sell ban jhankri T-shirts or memorabilia, whereas the yeti is commercially omnipresent. Yet there are no shrines or religious sites for the yeti, whereas there are a few for the ban jhankri to which shamans will pilgrimage and make offerings (e.g., Kalinchowk) (Miller 1997, 21), and ban jhankri cave sites that are thought to be their homes (e.g., Sailung in Dolakha district and Syangja near Pokhara). Shamans make dough images of the ban jhankri for their altars in order to invoke his spirit, but I have never seen any for the yeti. Further, there are literally scores of names for each, and although some of these names overlap, as mentioned above, most do not; therefore, it is easy to lose the thread connecting them (see Sanderson 1961, 454). However, Nepalese scholars, folklorists, and interested persons have made the connection.

On more than one occasion, two people told me a story that was identical in every major detail except that, in one telling, it was the ban jhankri who was the protagonist and, in the other, it was the small yeti. These identical renderings of folktales first alerted me to their potential identity. Indeed, their mythologies share a plethora of common features.

The ban jhankri, who abducts worthy shaman candidates in order to teach them, like the yeti that tests pure-hearted reclusive yogi, conveys its wisdom in the Himalayan forests and caves. Like the small yeti, the ban jhankri are male. Both males are considered *ban manche* (forest men) or *jangali* (wild), as well as spirits or deities. They are half-simian/half-human with the same height and colors. Both have cannibalistic, ferocious wives who are bigger than they are, with long breasts slung over their napes, who can be outrun going downhill (Peters 1981, 80–81; Peters 1982, 23–25; Riboli 2000, 84). Further, the ban jhankrini are called nyalmo; that is to say, nyalmo is the name many Tibetan people use for the female ban jhankri (ban jhankrini) (cf. Gupta and Nath 1994, 45–47, 100–101; Lall 1988a, 25; Wangdi 1994, 23). Both ban jhankri and small yeti have conical heads and hair covering their bodies except for face and hands. Both have amorous propensities toward their human abductees.

Ban jhankri are further similar to yeti in that their feet turn backward (Miller 1997, 216; Riboli 2000, 85) and they sometimes eat with the backs of their hands (Peters 1982, 23; 1997a, 59–60). Also they are nocturnal, have sharp night vision, and typically capture their victims after sundown. Similarly, neither typically wears clothes, and both demand that their abductees also be naked. Like yeti, ban jhankri perform full-moon rituals, community rituals, and divination. Similarly, they both possess many human attributes, and live for hundreds of years. Both can communicate to humans telepathically and emit high-pitched whistles and cries. Like yeti, ban jhankri bones possess healing and protective attributes (Conton 2001, 32; Macdonald 1976, 339 n. 67). I was told stories about ban jhankri who raid farms for milk and grain just like yeti. It is said both are nearly extinct as a result of human aggression, and that a fondness for alcohol has hastened the demise of the ban jhankri just as it has for the yeti.

Like small yeti, the ban jhankri may "attack" if provoked, and cause a person to become deaf, dumb, paralytic, or crazy. Both can possess their victims, causing them to shake and wander about aimlessly in the forest (Desjarlais 1992, 20–21, 94; Riboli 2000, 86). Thus, both ban jhankri and yeti are dangerous to encounter but, at the same time, are teachers for shamans or yogi. Further, it seems ban jhankri, like yeti, have been sighted only by indigenous people. Because of these many common features, Nepalese scholars and folklorists classify the ban jhankri either as a type of yeti (Gupta and Nath 1994, 46) or as having a "kindred" nature (Lall 1988a, 23). The former is more in line with my view, i.e., ban jhankri is a widely used Nepali term for the male yeti, emphasizing his spiritual shamanic powers.

THE SPIRIT OF THE *YETI*

The sources and perspectives of those interested in yeti lore are quite different from those researching the shamanism of the ban jhankri. Yeti lore and sightings are of interest to the Nepalese lay public and to Western expeditionists, as both groups seek to confirm the yeti's physical "ordinary reality" (O.R.)[46] existence, whereas the ban jhankri's oral mythology is derived primarily from the personal accounts of shamans' initiatory experiences recorded by anthropologists and other scholars who typically view these as N.O.R. encounters. The foci of these perspectives are distinct. Whereas the earlier O.R. studies described footprints and fleeting glimpses, the recent investigations are based on personal accounts of close-up, face-to-face interactions of shaman candidates with ban jhankri teachers. The shift to concern with N.O.R. also represents a shift of attention to the spiritual aspects of the ban jhankri and ban jhankrini. The "nonordinary" is the realm of spirit encounter. Therefore, the N.O.R. perspective accepts as valuable the very experiences of the natives with the yeti that Westerners desiring O.R. validation would tend to dismiss as superstition, fantasy, or dream.

To the Sherpa, the "yeti" scalp and other "relics" kept in their monasteries have a spiritual and practical ritual value. They are not there as empirical evidence. They function in Buddhist costumed and masked dance ceremonies (Fürer-Haimendorf 1964, 202; Nebesky-Wojkowitz 1993, 507–508) to invoke and embody spirit, which is why they are sacred objects and therefore possess a reality apart from being validated paleoanthropologically, i.e., in O.R. Marlin Perkins, the zoologist on the 1960 Hillary expedition, commissioned a Sherpa to fabricate a yeti scalp from a goatskin, after which he observed that the artist revered his creation as though it were a holy relic (Napier 1973, 56).

That the yeti is a numinous figure seems obvious. In fact, the Sherpa believe that the community is in jeopardy if yeti sacra are disrespected or lost (Messner 2000, 63). Still, the spiritual character of the yeti is not generally understood. Thus, while the yeti has an important role in Buddhist sacred dances like the Mani Rimdu (roughly translated "all will be well" [Messner 2000, 32]), the meaning of that role is obscure and the Sherpa are able to say only that his presence is prescribed by custom (Fürer-Haimendorf 1964, 202). In my opinion, this is because the yeti's role in the great monastic dances is fundamentally alien to

Buddhist precepts. In the dance, two men are costumed as yeti, with fur robes and conical skullcaps, carrying bow and arrow and small, round shields. They accompany the chief lama outside the village boundary, where they sacrifice the "enemy," a small, human-like image made of flour and water that has come to embody the ills of the community and is to be used as a scapegoat (Tibetan: *lüd*). The yeti participants are called the "killers" (Sherpa: *gemaka*) and carry the guilt for the murder (sacrifice) of the scapegoat, even though it is the lama who shoots the arrow (Fürer-Haimendorf 1964, 202–203). The rinpoché, the learned lama, exonerate themselves of responsibility for the killing in the dance performance with an esoteric explanation that turns the shooting of the arrow into a sacred positive event that releases the soul of the demon held in the scapegoat so it can ascend to paradise and/or find liberation (Kohn 2001, 80–85).

On the other hand, the yeti in the performance described by Fürer-Haimendorf (1964, 185–208) appear to be hunters betraying their ancient origins, and carry the stigma as the murderers, who, unlike Buddhists, take life and eat the meat of the animals they kill. This is why it would appear that those paid to play yeti in the ceremonial dances are generally from another group or of the poor, lower-socioeconomic status, because this role in the performance is not particularly desirable. Those costumed as the yeti are called killers because of the Buddhist view of sacrifice. However, sacrifice was a prominent feature of ancient Bönpo shamanism. In fact, the yeti embodying the role of the killers parallels the ritual role of the chief Bön shamans (Tibetan: *shen*) of ancient Tibet (Ekvall 1964, 20–21, 28–29). In other words, hidden in the Buddhist performance are the ancient shamanic origins of the yeti.

According to Buddhist legend, Guru Rinpoche (or, in some versions, Milarepa) triumphed over the Bön ancestral shaman Nara Bön in a contest flying up a mountain, and thereafter the Buddhist lama replaced the Bön shaman in their spiritual duties. As told in some versions of the story, the contest between the two (Bönpo and Buddhist) was required because, according to Guru Rinpoche, "souls were not reaching heaven." Apparently, the shamans did not have the moral power to accomplish this, because they make blood sacrifices (Chang 1962, 220–222, 247; Peters 1981, 57). However, the Mani Rimdu and Buddhist New Year dance ceremonies, like some others, are, in essence, sacrificial rites and therefore not the province of orthodox Buddhism but of shamanism.

Such "sacrificial" Buddhist ceremonies are very similar to the exorcism rites practiced by Himalayan tribal shamans, in which scapegoats are sacrificed as ransom (the literal meaning of *lüd*) to the evil spirits in order to release the patient and allow healing (Nebesky-Wojkowitz 1993, 507–513; Peters 1995, 56–57; 2000, 23–24). Thus, Bönpo practices such as these have persisted into modern times, and the shamans of the tribal Tibetan groups have maintained these practices as part of a tradition existing alongside, and unassimilated by, Buddhism (Ekvall 1964, 17). This shamanic Bön tradition is supported by its own oral mythology that articulates its own separate area of religious expertise.

There are different endings to the story of the flying contest between the Buddhist hero and the Bön shaman depending on group affiliation. In the Buddhist version, as related above, Milarepa or Guru Rinpoche is the clear-cut victor (Chang 1962, 220–222); in another group's version, Nara Bön is the winner (Hoffmann 1961, 25, 99). The Tamang shamans with whom I conducted ethnographic research in the Kathmandu Valley end the story as a draw. Thus, they say the lama preside over funerals because they alone know how to liberate souls from the world, whereas the shamans know how to ransom the demons of disease and therefore have retained responsibility for healing and making sacrifices (cf. Oppitz 1998, 51; Peters 1981, 55–58).

The completely separate existence of the shamanism and Lamaism that I discovered among the tribal Tamang is not the case for those shamans who fled Tibet after the Chinese invasion of the 1950s and now reside in Tibetan refugee camps in Nepal, whose work is sanctioned by the Buddhist hierarchy (Berglie 1976, 93; Sifers and Peters 2001, 32). These shamans do not practice sacrifice as do the ethnic Tibetan Himalayan tribal groups of Nepal.

There are other differences between the two spiritualities, other than sacrifice, that are articulated in legend. From the perspective of bombo legends of the Tamang, lama have a completely different relationship to souls and spirits than shamans. Lama read from books (e.g., *The Tibetan Book of the Dead*) in order to guide souls of persons who have died from this earthly realm. Bombo, on the other hand, have no books. They have no need for them, as they confront the spirits "face-to-face," "play" with them, and negotiate with them in order to heal their patients; that is to say, they have a direct relationship (cf. Peters 1981, 60, 126–127).

Another important difference is that shamanism fosters "harmony" with animistic nature. From my experiences, it is concerned with a person's earthly relationships to spirits, animals, and other humans in the here and now, as opposed to liberation of the soul from the world of suffering (see Mumford 1989, 113–115). It is in the ancient Bönpo belief system of the Tibetan tribal peoples whose shamanic practice has resisted Buddhist assimilation and whose shamans still speak directly to the nature spirits of the mountains and forests that the trail of the yeti must be sought.

I have already pointed out some of the strong assertions of the yeti's spirit nature found in folklore and that these legends correspond in many respects to those of the ban jhankri. From the standpoint of nomenclature, it was shown that there is obvious correlation in their identity, as the small yeti is called rang shi bombo in the Tibetan languages. Again, bombo in Tamang, bönpo in Tibetan, like jhankri in Nepali, means shaman. Tibeto-speaking shamans like the Tamang say the ban jhankri is also a *rang shi tugpa*. As mentioned regarding the yeti, rang shi means "spontaneously" or "self-generated," i.e., a being that arises out of itself, independently and without external constraint or stimulus. Nepali shamans say the ban jhankri appears to his candidates *aph se aph;* that is to say, naturally and automatically, without the candidate's desire, design, or effort. Such spontaneous manifestation (rang shi) is thus another common characteristic of both the yeti and ban jhankri. *Tugpa* means tutelary or teaching spirit, so that rang shi tugpa can be translated as "spontaneously arising tutelary spirit" and is a good description of the initiatory encounter between the ban jhankri and the unsuspecting young shaman candidate (cf. Hitchcock 1976, 169, 173; Peters 1981, 62).

Things that arise spontaneously are considered holy and carry a miraculous connotation. Many of the holiest shrines and temples are situated on hills (e.g., Swayambu) or have sacred images of deities (e.g., Ganesh and Saraswati at Pharping, and Shiva at Richeswar [near Daman]) that are said to have arisen spontaneously and unexpectedly from large stones. Such spontaneous self-generation has sacred value as it connotes the object embodies the spiritual power of the divine. It is a key characteristic of the Tibetan Buddhas (deities) and, as discussed earlier, of the ban jhankri and yeti (Anderson 1975, 331–332; Bajracharya 1985, 2; Slusser 1998, 276, 298; Snellgrove 1957, 95). Because the initiate shaman's encounter with and abduction by the ban jhankri has this spontaneous quality, these shamans are considered to be the most powerful. In Nepal, people believe that such a shamanic "calling" is a mark of distinction and confers unofficial status to the initiates. In fact, those initiated by the ban jhankri identify themselves as ban jhankri; that is, ban jhankri abductees.

Traditionally, the Tamang say that there are seven different types of ban jhankri forest spirits, but I have been able to learn about only two of these: the *sunna* (golden) ban jhankri and the *laato* (dumb) ban jhankri. One of the Magar shamans with whom I work identifies himself as a *sunna jhankri.* Sunna jhankri forest spirits are considered to be descendants of the sun deity, as well as legendary guardians of gold, protecting and inhabiting the cavernous tunnels where gold, the incorruptible metal of incalculable wealth, is believed hidden. However, all types of ban jhankri emanate from the pristine Golden or Truth Era. All have golden drums and, in some descriptions, the female carries a golden sword, sacred objects that harken back to the Golden Era when men and animals spoke the same language, a time before the "veils" dropped that now separate humans and deities, heaven and earth, a time before the low morals and defilement of the present Dark Age or Kali Yuga (see Zimmer 1972, 13–15).

In one ban jhankri folk story, Shiva, unable to find anyone in the cities who was "pure" and therefore worthy to receive his sacred teachings, found a young boy living in the sacred forest uncontaminated by urban corruption. The young boy was named Laato, a word that means developmentally slow or simple, and especially unable to speak normally (Peters 1980, 352). In this context, laato is not used pejoratively, but rather means innocent and unspoiled by sophisticated city life and the caste system (Macdonald 1976, 321, 336 n. 54, 337 n. 57). When Tamang shamans are embodied by the laato ban jhankri, they do not speak, but rather grunt, whistle, nod, and point. Even though the boy is purely human, in this story he is wild and uncivilized. But he is also powerful, having the ability to invoke Bhairab (a terrifying and monstrous form of Shiva) in order to have control over sorcerers and ghosts (Macdonald 1976, 337 n. 57). In the forest, Shiva taught the boy the art of shamanizing and healing and initiated him as his first ban jhankri, instructing him to follow his model and to bring those likewise worthy and pure of heart into the forests and caves and teach them. From that time on, those who were ill could seek shamanic help. Ban jhankri abductions and initiations fulfill and are validated by such legends (see Macdonald 1976, 321–322).

The Tibetan anthropogeny discussed earlier tells of the half-human, small wildmen forest ancestors. In the Buddhist renderings of the story, they are "cultural heroes" as "in the beginning" under the tutelage of the compassionate Chenrezig, the wildmen took rains from the forest and developed agriculture. In the process, the forefathers dropped their monkey tails (i.e., the connection to their animal origins) and became civilized, domesticated, and "tamed," as life no longer focused on the ancient forest and its spirit but, rather, became centralized around Buddhist faith and its great monastic urban theocracies, which were also the centers of the economy and education (Samuel 1993, 19–21, 167–173; Shakabpa 1967, 13–14, 21–22).

The earliest prehistoric phase of Tibetan spirituality is that of "primitive Bön," otherwise known as "black Bön" or "revealed Bön," to differentiate it from "white Bön." The latter, like Buddhism, is monastic and assimilated a large portion of Buddhist literature. Black Bön is shamanic and has, as already noted, an oral tradition (Li 1948, 35–36; Schuhmacher and Woerner 1989, 41–42), probably many thousands of years old, as it contains several elements in common with the ancient shamanism of Siberia, shamanism's classic locus (Eliade 1964, 504; Nebesky-Wojkowitz 1993, 541–553). As mentioned earlier, it is also a current and tenacious spiritual practice, even in large cities like Kathmandu and, while influenced by Buddhism and Hinduism, still contains many prehistoric Bön rituals and beliefs that reflect an old, predominantly pastoral, nomadic and hunting culture. One of these is sacrifice and another is the importance given to the mountain and forest deities, which are not representative of the settled agricultural Buddhists (Spindler and Spindler 1968, vi).

In other words, before Buddhism civilized shamanism, the spirits of the mountains and forests were sacred. The term *göd* (from *me* or *mi-göd,* yeti or wildman) means "not subdued," "not domesticated," "natural," and "untamed," and is imbued with positive value and considered a compliment by Tibetan nomads (Ekvall 1968, 92–93) but is less compatible with monks and agriculturalists (Samuel 1993, 218, 222). Ekvall (1968, 93) writes of göd: "the term probably says most aptly what the culture hero should be … [the Tibetan nomads] prefer to be known as 'untamed'" (brackets mine).

Such an ideal personality and ethos is different from the Buddhist version of the monkey/man culture heroes who brought agriculture and then became fully human. Originally, the yeti were untamed and wild creatures of the forests and mountains and, before agriculture was dominant, were fierce deities who needed propitiation, as life and nourishment (i.e., the hunt) depended on them.

Thus, to be abducted by them is to return to origins, to the sacred source of power and wisdom of the untamed, of the unhewn forested mountains. And to be initiated by this wild wisdom is to be initiated by the half-animal divine spirits of the forests and mountains. However, not everyone who is spontaneously called to the mysterious forest is up to such a dangerous encounter.

FAILED INITIATORY ENCOUNTERS WITH *BAN JHANKRI*

Case Study #1: Those whom the ban jhankri finds "imperfect" are not initiated, as in the case of Giri, a forty-year-old Tamang woman I met in Boudha. She relates that, early one evening when she was seven years old, she was walking in the forest with her father. When her father wasn't looking, a ban jhankri jumped out from behind some thickets and grabbed her. Overcome with fear and confusion, Giri was taken through the forest to the ban jhankri's cave, where he took off her clothes and had sex with her. Afterward, he inspected Giri and noticed a small scar on her face, an imperfection for which he decided not to teach her, and "threw" her out of the cave. She returned home unclothed and traumatized. However, because they were "married," the ban jhankri has not left Giri spiritually. He continues to possess her, causing her to shake uncontrollably. During the one day and night she spent with him, Giri learned invocation mantra, but she does not know how to keep the ban jhankri in its "proper place" so that he does not continue to come at inopportune times. When she attempts to "play" him—that is, invoke him—he makes her shake out of control and causes her distress. Giri is not considered a shaman. Currently she wants the ban jhankri to give her mantra to use against an ex-husband and avenge his abuse. The ban jhankri has not responded. Neither shamans nor doctors seem to be able to help her more than temporarily.

Case Study #2: Baktabahadur, a thirty-year-old Tamang man from the area near Boudha, was also taken as a seven-year-old and kept for one day. The ban jhankri tried to teach him mantra, but he couldn't focus and memorize them. Thus, the ban jhankri got angry and "threw" him. Baktabahadur says he literally flew out of the cave, hitting a huge rock that seriously slashed his lip. He spent days in the hospital and still wears the scar, not only of the physical wound but of the psychologically traumatic encounter with the ban jhankri teacher, who possesses him to this day and makes him shake, just as with Giri. Because Baktabahadur is not a healer, most people, including his wife, think he is crazy. When the ban jhankri possesses Baktabahadur, he speaks through him and identifies himself, but says nothing that has meaning after that. Consequently, it is understood as a "ban jhankri illness" and not an initiation.

I have spoken with shamans who have been "thrown" by ban jhankri on the first day because of some defect. One passed gas; another became ill and fainted when he was kidnapped. These men, one a Hindu of the tailor caste and the other a Tamang, now function as shamans in their communities. The ban jhankri embodies them, but in a more controlled possession-trance than Baktabahadur and Giri experience, because these men studied with an O.R. guru who initiated them and taught them how to develop N.O.R. relations with their ban jhankri and conduct shamanic healing rituals. And, while it is true that these practicing shamans call themselves ban jhankri shamans because they "play" with the ban jhankri spirit, they are not actually his initiates. They themselves say that they were not "completed" by the ban jhankri. They were "thrown" before finishing the entire experiential process as related in the ban jhankri myth and as told by other ban jhankri initiated shamans.

Part of the ban jhankri encounter entails the inspection of the body and the heart-mind (man) of the novice for any spiritual impurities or pollution (jutho). Beliefs about jutho are nearly all-pervasive. Things too numerous to list are either jutho (polluted, profane) or *chokho* (pure, sacred). In the initiatory ban jhankri encounter, abductees may be rejected due to a body scar (a sign of imperfection), as with Giri, or actions considered indications of spiritual deficiency, like passing gas, inattention, or becoming ill, as in the other examples. Macdonald (1976, 323) writes of the ban jhankri of Muglan, in India adjacent to Nepal: "They choose young men ... who suffer neither from skin diseases, bowel disorders, nor burns...." Such conditions are evaluated as jutho by the ban jhankri and are therefore incompatible with initiation. Sometimes the ban jhankri will cleanse and purify the novice before training (Riboli 2000, 86–90). However, in the cases cited above, he chose not to, for reasons known only to him.

In the context of the ban jhankri's inspection of the heart-mind (man), it is the candidate's intrinsic values, morals, and propensity to do good that are being evaluated. In other words, the ban jhankri is making a value judgment as to the nature of the child candidate's character, just as yeti do with yogi. "Is his heart-mind chokho or is it jutho?" Jutho characters in the extreme are sorcerers. Their work is antithetical to healing life, and to the purifying/cleansing work done by shamans. Instead, sorcerers "spoil" life through deception and betrayal. Those with "black" (jutho, mendacious, malicious, sorcerous) man are deemed unworthy to receive teaching and initiation and are consequently not "chosen" to be ban jhankri. If abducted, they are soon "thrown" by the ban jhankri when he comes to know the quality of the candidate's heart-mind.

SUCCESSFUL INITIATORY ENCOUNTERS WITH *BAN JHANKRI*

Case Study #3: Most agree that the maximum amount of time to study with the ban jhankri is thirty days. Any more time risks capture by the ban jhankrini and is deemed superfluous. Reports in the literature vary; and some shamans talk of three-, five-, seven-, or nine-day ordeals. Many are abducted a number of times. A very few speak in terms of years. Gajendra, my Tamang shaman teacher in the mid-1970s, said he spent a total of seven days with the ban jhankri who abducted him four or five times when he was thirteen. Initially, Gajendra had been acting "crazy," periodically shaking uncontrollably. At times he was mute, was highly anxious, couldn't sleep, and lost his appetite. During the episodes, his parents cared for his personal hygiene. Then one day, six months after these episodes started, Gajendra began shaking, tore off his clothes, and ran naked into the forest, where he stayed for three days. He had been "possessed" by the spirit of his grandfather, a well-regarded shaman and ban jhankri initiate who had died nine years earlier, and taken to the ban jhankri. In the forest, he encountered many ban jhankri and their ban jhankrini wives with his grandfather. The ban jhankri gave Gajendra earthworms and tree bark as food, threatening that he would die if he didn't eat it. When he went to take the food to his mouth, the ban jhankrini whipped his hands and bellowed, "Let's cut off his head." Sometimes she waved her golden sword menacingly. But the ban jhankri said, "No," as he wanted to teach Gajendra, having found him to be pure of heart. Gajendra was first taught to take the food with the back of his hands, a ritual technique shamans typically use with their patients to fend off sorcerers and bad-spirit attacks. After Gajendra learned how to do this, the ban jhankrini was unable to harm him. Thereafter, even when relaxing between teachings, Gajendra was protected from the ban jhankrini by the ban jhankri or his grandfather, who would stand in front of him whenever the ban jhankrini lunged at him.

Gajendra described the ban jhankrini or nyalmo, as he called them in Tamang, as tall, furry, black, bear-like beasts with big teeth and breasts that hung below the waist. The ban jhankri were only three feet tall, with red hair covering their bodies, and pointed caps.

After his initial teachings, Gajendra wandered aimlessly in the forest. He heard vicious dogs barking that chased after him, who turned out to be his parents and other villagers calling to him. Finally, they caught up with him and took him home.

Gajendra described the experience as dream-like. He said he "woke up" and "stopped shivering" when he returned home. But the very same night, he was taken by his grandfather for a second time. He said a path opened up for him that was invisible to anyone who might attempt to follow him into the forest. Again he was naked but, this time, armed with his father's (also a shaman) magical dagger (Tibetan: phurba). In the forest, he was pursued by numerous demons led by the nyalmo. Some had no heads, and had eyes in the middle of their chests; others had large jaws and three red eyes. He ran down a mountain, knowing from childhood legend this was the best way to escape the nyalmo. Still, he was cornered in a cremation ground. Other demons carrying corpses and death flags attacked him there. They held him down and began devouring his body. His skeleton was exposed as the demons tore at his flesh with spades, picks, claws, and teeth. He felt as though he had come to the cemetery to die, and cried out in fear to Shiva to save him. "Bhagwan, I am only a young boy and I don't want to die!" He tried to defend himself with the phurba, but the metal dagger fell from his hands and struck a rock, where it created a spark of light. Instantly the experience ended, the demons disappeared, and Gajendra was saved. He "woke up" in the cemetery area and returned home with morning's first light.

At least two more abductions followed. I'm not sure precisely how to separate which parts of these encounters with the ban jhankri were dream experiences, journeys or visions during shaking episodes (i.e., possession-trances), or actual forest wanderings, or mixtures of these. During one of these encounters, the ban jhankri gave Gajendra an initiation and mantra that enabled him to master fire and heat. In another, he was tested by having to put his hands in boiling oil and sit on beds of live coals. In perhaps others, the ban jhankri introduced Gajendra to a tiger power animal that did healing "extractions." He also taught Gajendra to play the ban jhankri's golden drum, and "fly from mountain peak to mountain peak." The result of these teachings provided Gajendra with powerful skills that he used throughout his later life as a shaman, to heal his patients.[47]

After these encounters, Gajendra's deceased grandfather became his chief tutelary spirit. Gajendra also served a nine-year apprenticeship under his maternal uncle, an accomplished ban jhankri shaman. Gajendra was considered to be a ban jhankri (rang shi bombo) initiate. He continued to "play" with the ban jhankri spirit, whom he invoked during rituals and for whom he left offerings and made effigies of flour (Tibetan: *torma*) on his altar.[48]

Case Study #4: Ram Ali, a young man in his twenties, a Magar ban jhankri shaman I met in the Pokhara area of Nepal, was taken when he was nine years old. Earlier, he had dreams in which a ban jhankri came to him and said he would return one day and teach him to be a shaman. Still, when the day arrived, Ram was surprised. He was picking fruit near his village when the ban jhankri suddenly appeared and said, "So you've come to eat," giving Ram a few fruits to eat that instantly put him into a dream-like state.

Ram relates that the wind began to blow like a tornado, and there was a big storm accompanied by an earthquake. The ban jhankri took him to his cave, which he entered by crawling through a small hole. Ram says he spent four years with the ban jhankri and his wife, whom Ram describes as bear-like and calls nyalmo. Other shamans question the validity of four years, but Ram says he never wanted to leave. It was a palatial golden cave. He says it was like being in a dream and he wanted for nothing. Still, while there, he ate worms with the backs of his hands, under the threat of being killed and cannibalized by the golden-sword-wielding ban jhankrini. Similar to Gajendra, Ram describes the ban jhankri as small, golden, hairy, looking like a monkey, and able to appear and disappear mysteriously and shape-shift at will. He had long, white hair with a pointed cap made of gold and diamonds. The ban jhankri taught Ram many powerful mantra and then returned him to where he had initially abducted him years earlier. The ban jhankri still appears in Ram's dreams and in shamanic states of consciousness, and instructs him. When conducting shamanic healings, Ram invokes the ban jhankri as his chief teaching spirit. After this experience, Ram found an experienced ban jhankri shaman initiate to be his O.R. guru.

After abduction and teaching, candidates take the ban jhankri as one of their chief tutelary spirits. The ban jhankri continues to teach his disciples in dreams, and embody and instruct them during ritual. But the initiates also (in all but a few examples) learn from an external O.R. guru after they are returned.

THE *NYALMO* OR *BAN JHANKRINI*[49]

The ban jhankrini or nyalmo yeti, like the rock ogress that spawned the Tibetan people, are fierce and demonic presences. In the taming process of Buddhism, as was discussed earlier, the original wild and fierce mountain deities/demons were assimilated as dharmapala or protectors of the faith. The rock ogress became an emanation of Tara; the monkey became her bodhisattva consort. Another demon (sin-mo), of the same type as the rock ogress, was defeated by Srong Tsan Gampo, the hero king and first Buddhist king of Tibet (Samuel 1993, 168). This defeat by magical means needed to occur before Srong Tsan Gampo could propagate the *dharma* to his people. A Buddhist version of this story of the first ogress comes from a Tibetan *terma* (revealed or discovered) text (*Mani Kabum*), which also contains the Buddhist account of the second sin-mo, whose body corresponds to the landscape of central

Tibet and who was "nailed down" by erecting temples and monasteries on her various body parts. Her heart lies below the royal capital of Lhasa (Samuel 1993, 168).

This story is significant because it symbolizes an important "turning point" in Tibetan history, the ascension of Buddhism (Tucci 1988, 168–169) by securing control of the pre-Buddhist Bön mountain and nature goddesses (Dowman 1988, 285).

As the nyalmo is a representative of the aboriginal past, she therefore has many features in common with both of these fierce sin-mo goddesses, especially the first, as she has not been "nailed down." As set forth above, neither the nyalmo nor her forest wildman mate has been incorporated into Buddhism. The first sin-mo was interpreted as a Tara but, as the yeti, she has developed an independent folkloric existence. That is, yeti continue to exist in folklore and the oral shamanic tradition. They are unassimilated but not uninfluenced, as the yeti is a living folktale. It has many modern anecdotes, and there are new encounters and new stories about them developing all the time (Lall 1988a, 30–55). In fact, yeti folklore in the Kathmandu Valley has assimilated some of the deities of Hinduism into its own sphere. For example, as discussed, the ban jhankri becomes a disciple of Shiva; the nyalmo is seen as a Kali. There is a certain wisdom in this, as there is much overlap, especially in the Shiva-Kali partnership (see below). However, the ban jhankri yeti and the nyalmo yeti have their own story to tell, and this is, as I have argued, the story of becoming a shaman.

Like the ban jhankri, his partner the ban jhankrini is a notable element of the shamanic initiatory experience. Most "complete" ban jhankri shamans have an encounter with her. All the shamans, as well as interested Nepali, say she lives with the ban jhankri in their cave. Scholars, when summarizing the experience, typically include the large, dangerous, cannibalizing bear-woman in their descriptions (Desjarlais 1989, 195; Miller 1997, 219; Skafte 1992, 50). According to some researchers, they are "inseparable" (Riboli 2000, 84).

If not for her, the shaman's initiation would lose much of the necessary element of danger and therefore be less of a trial. She threatens the candidate's life, to dismember and devour him. In Gajendra's encounter, she orchestrated his "dismemberment" and "skeletonization" and thus his "death" and "rebirth" as a shaman (Eliade 1964, 63–64, 66). Aside from physical death, she presents the psychic danger of sexually enslaving the male candidate, holding him a prisoner and stealing his life energy. She does not teach, like the ban jhankri. The nyalmo tests and challenges the future shaman's resolve to learn by threatening his very existence.

The marital union of the ban jhankri and ban jhankrini is a bringing together of opposites. She is big; he is small. She is dark; he is light. She is violent and rageful; he is a teacher who does not present a danger but protects his "pure" candidates. She is said to leave the cave every evening and return the next morning. If she smells her husband's disciples, she demands a slice of flesh, threatening to cut off their heads, fingers, and toes with her weapon and to cannibalize them. However, the ban jhankri refuses his wife's demand for his candidates' lives (Eigner 2001, 27). He will protect and hide the novices and teach them to become invisible, or perform ritual gestures to ward her off, or perhaps lock her in an iron cage. If candidates are lazy and not studious, he may threaten to let her devour them (Riboli 2000, 88). In some accounts, the ban jhankri is said to teach his abductees in a separate room, where his wife is not allowed, so that she cannot overhear the mantra he teaches and wreak havoc upon the world (Skafte 1992, 50). One shaman told me that the ban jhankri is especially careful not to "transmit" the *OM* mantra of Shiva, the mantra of world creation, from his mouth to her ears. If he did, she would turn it into its opposite, strip it of its healing effects, and eventually destroy the world.

This nefarious tendency to work against life connects the ban jhankrini with other such beings, like the yakshini of Hindu lore mentioned above and the bokshi (female sorcerers or "witches"). There are *boksha* too, male sorcerers, but it is believed they are not imbued with as much evil power, as bokshi will sacrifice their children for power (see Peters 1997a, 57). In fact, she is known as Queen of Sorcerers while the ban jhankri is known as the King of Shamans.

Shamans and bokshi are polar opposites. They are in constant combat, as shamans' work is to prolong life, but the bokshi bring illness, enmity, calamity, and death. The ban jhankri and ban jhankrini are an odd couple indeed. Still, they have been a team, initiating shamans together, since the Beginning. I believe that underlying their apparent opposition, there is an interdependence and complementarity. Indeed, shamans say, "without bokshi there would be no shamans."

A story told by two Magar shamans from Pokhara, Bel and Sumendra Thapa, explains the relationship of shamans and sorcerers:

· The Work of Shamans and Bokshi ·

There were nine bokshi sisters and their younger brother, a shaman. The shaman brother was building a house and was on the roof. His eldest sister felt envy and gave him the evil eye, causing him to fall and die. In the afterworld, the shaman met his tutelary guru, who told him he would be resurrected in three days. Immediately thereafter he needed to prepare an offering of flat bread for his sisters, and one for himself: ten pieces in all. When the bread was presented to his sisters, they ate it voraciously. Spying his piece of bread, they attacked him to get it, so he threw it up in the air. Before it could come down, the nine sisters had vanquished one another, all except for the youngest, who lay exhausted on the floor. The shaman moved in to kill her, but stopped when she raised her hand to block his blow and said, "Do not kill me. If you do, you will not have a job. . . ."[50]

The teaching is that shamans and sorcerers work together by working against each other. They are necessary aspects of the same process.

Without sorcerers who create problems, there would be no need for shamans who resolve them. The story continues that, without shamans to make substitute offerings so that their patients' lives can be extended, sorcerers would soon exhaust human life due to their unmitigated voracious bloodlust. Consequently, in the end, they couldn't do their murderous, cannibalistic work. Thus the two are complementary: evil and good, sorcerer-queen and shaman-king, ban jhankrini and ban jhankri. Without one, there couldn't be the other. Each is a necessary component of the interdependence of opposites.

As was noted, the ban jhankrini, like the nyalmo, is thought to be a ban kali (forest Kali), a dark, destructive, and fierce forest goddess who is often seen as a huntress and nature goddess. She is the destructive, but necessary, part of nature, and shamans honor her and her hunter spirits. Kali is the death-wielding goddess wife of Shiva. She is often imaged as a terrifying, emaciated crone carrying a sword and wearing a garland of human skulls (Mookerjee 1988, 62). In one story, she is in a horrible rage, killing everyone and everything in her sight, her protruding tongue dripping blood. None of the deities knew how to break her destructive state of consciousness and feared she would destroy the world before long. In desperation, they called upon Shiva, who, acknowledging their plea, developed a plan and, taking the appearance of a corpse, lay down in Kali's path. When she came to him, consumed by her rage, she failed to see his outstretched body across her path, stumbled, and briefly lost her balance. Regaining her footing, she looked around to see what had broken her stride. Seeing Shiva on the ground, she thought, "Oh no! I have killed my husband!" and immediately stopped her rampage. Thus Shiva saved the world from death and destruction by disrupting Kali's furious state of consciousness (Pattanaik 1977, 64–65).

The ban jhankrini is that part of nature, the ban kali huntress, the destructive Mother Goddess, the dark but necessary part that, by bringing death, nourishes all of life. She is nature, and nature eats nature in order to survive (Caldwell 1999, 112–114). The ban jhankri, follower of Shiva, reveals the opposite. His spirit teaches how to control the ban jhankrini and postpone her work, her inevitable process of death, if only temporarily, by abducting youths, taking them away from their familiar surroundings and into the sacred forests and caves in order to teach the worthy among them the practice of shamanism.

CONCLUSION

In the beginning, yeti was a disparaging nickname, an epithet directed at the sin-mo, the cannibalistic rock demoness who, I believe, became not only Tara for the Buddhists but also the yeti, who, over time, developed its own folkloric identity. The function of the rock ogress in Tibetan aboriginal culture cannot be ascertained with certainty. It can be surmised, however, from ancient texts and current ethnography. From these sources, it is known that she was rageful, sexual, and cannibalistic; a voracious monster and the Queen of Sorcerers and ghosts, who are the agents of disease, disorder, and death. The teaching of the male ban jhankri, himself deeply immersed in wild and spontaneous nature, initiates the candidate into the ritual and sacred methods to contain her and her frightening entourage. The candidate learns to fly, gains mastery over fire, and acquires mantra with which to invoke deities and expel demons. Traditionally, the shamans offer sacrifice, satiating the demons by giving a ransom in exchange for the patient. Spiritual illness is typically thought to be an attack by hungry spirits feasting on the patient. From this perspective, illness is the result of spiritual cannibalism, and the accomplished shaman knows how to become master over the cannibalistic demons of disease.

Buddhist meditation is an attempt to permanently change the practitioner's consciousness: to attain a final unity of compassion, wisdom, and nonattachment. Shamanic practices, on the other hand, have a more limited healing purpose. According to Eliade (1964, 416–417), the aim of the yoga practices basic to Tantric Hinduism and Buddhism is "enstasis," which is the "... final concentration of the Spirit and 'escape' from the cosmos." Shamanism is "structurally" distinct in that its "... final goal is always 'ecstasy,' the soul's ecstatic journey...." The difference is a temporary ecstatic trance, as opposed to a permanent invulnerable, adamantine enstasis. The latter is the result of following an initiatory road map for developing nonattachment and selfless, compassionate consciousness, whereas the former is a specific trance state, often described as "seeing," that involves a vision journey into N.O.R., followed by a return to the ordinary state of consciousness (see Harner 1990, 50).

As Samuel (1993, 595 n. 2) has noted, there is a close relationship between shamanism and Tantric practices, as they both employ visualization. The spontaneous visions arising in Buddhist meditation (Tucci 1961, 68–72) have many commonalities with the Bönpo shaman's ecstatic journey (Peters and Price-Williams 1983, 15–19). The candidate ban jhankri, like the Buddhist yogi, heroes, and saints, are tested and receive teaching directly from the spirits and deities while in hermitage in the Himalayan forest and mountain caves. Padma Sambhava and Milarepa were famous for their realizations attained in secluded caves. Like their shaman counterparts, the ban jhankri initiates, they must confront demonic presences and master them. In the twenty-eighth song of Milarepa (Chang 1962, 296–311), Milarepa describes his encounter with a cannibalistic demoness and her entourage of spirits who attacked him, saying:

> "We have come to confuse you and hurt you ...
>
> We have come to take your life, your soul, your spirit
>
> To stop your life and take your consciousness from your body
>
> To drink your blood and eat your flesh...."

Milarepa reflects:

"Especially fierce amongst them

Are the five cannibalistic demonesses

Who with abusive language curse me

And shout, 'Die you shall, you must!'"

(Chang 1962, 302–304)

From the perspective of Buddhist lore, one interpretation of the demonesses suggested by Chang (1962, 311 n. 3) is that they are wrathful emanations of a goddess who has come to test the understanding, resolve, and realization of the yogi and his ability to overcome fear. Such an interpretation is synchronous with the shaman's initiation, as discussed in earlier sections. The only distinction is that, in the Buddhist stories, the ancient, fierce mountain goddesses have been converted to fierce Buddhist goddesses. This is the theme found in yeti lore when the yeti goes to the yogi's or lama's cave, i.e., an encounter with a Buddhist deity and teacher. However, the deeper perspective of the Buddhist path and Milarepa's realization is that all demons and deities alike are "fictions of the mind." Milarepa writes:

"I do not fear you demons.

Fictions conjured up by mind.

Manifest yet non-existent...."

(Chang 1962, 304)

Once understood as illusions, they are no longer hindrances to liberation (Chang 1962, 304).

To the Bönpo, these demonic beings are real! They are the powerful spirits of nature, of the wilderness and mountains, and relationship with them is vital for maintaining harmony with the awesome presence of a sometimes-monstrous nature. Relationship with the deities and demons is developed and maintained in periods of ecstasy. In these temporary states of consciousness, the candidate shaman learns the techniques to contain these dark powers from the ban jhankri.

An important ritual technique that Gajendra learned from the ban jhankri on his first abduction was to accept the food he was given using both sides of his hands: both palms up and palms down. If he failed to do this, as mentioned earlier, the nyalmo whipped his hands and threatened to decapitate him and eat his flesh. The practice of taking food from both sides of the hands is called *ulto-sulto* (*ulto* = right way; *sulto* = contrary or opposite way). Ulto-sulto is a purification and ritual healing procedure that many bombo (not only ban jhankri initiates) use in healing ceremonies. Patients are instructed to eat ritually blessed food or herbal remedies from both sides of their hands to cure various spiritual disorders, in children as well as adults.

This simple ritual gesture is culturally believed to have far-reaching cosmic implications. The two sides of the hand are recognized, by analogy, to be the same as the positive and negative poles of existence: day/night, visible/invisible, good/evil, health/disease, male/female, shaman/sorcerer, ban jhankri/ban jhankrini, and more. By taking food to mouth palms down, the evil spirits and sorcerers, those agents of affliction who are commanded by their queen, the ban jhankrini or nyalmo yeti, are given an offering to satiate their cannibalistic lust for blood. By taking food palms up, the correct way, the deities' protective powers are invoked and called to action (cf. Peters 1997a, 59–61).

Ulto-sulto is an offering to both sides: negative and positive. The shamans recognize the value of honoring both sides, both demon and deity. This is an essential aspect of the shaman's relationship to spirits of all kinds. Thus, shamans have to keep a balance, a harmony between the cosmic forces of dark and light, illness and health, evil and good. Such balance, the guru say, keep the spirits in their "proper place."

Evolutionism-minded researchers theorized that the yeti was a pre-human link of significance in the chain of human development. But finding the yeti proved elusive. As previously mentioned, bones, furs, footprint casts, and other evidence of its O.R. existence failed to meet scientific scrutiny. Furthermore, as the worldwide hunt for a "missing link" led to a scientific dead-end, the yeti, who became associated with this search, fell into disrepute as a superstitious fallacy of the Himalayan natives. In other words, the yeti appeared to be a superstition wed to a spurious theory. Consequently, the yeti academically became an "abominable snowman." This view was further reinforced in the 1960s, when, except for the work of a few anthropologists like Napier (1973) and Shackley (1983), Hillary and others scathingly debunked and finally assassinated the yeti, as far as any remaining serious research into its O.R. existence (Coleman 1989, 101).

Meanwhile, after cultural anthropology was released from the shackles of an evolutionism paradigm, anthropologists interested in the shamanism of the Himalaya began recording the personal accounts of shamans who had encountered the ban jhankri. That the ban jhankri is a yeti seemingly escaped this scholarly reflection. As discussed above, Nepalese folklorists recognize the ban jhankri as either a yeti-type or a kindred being; at least one Western scholar acknowledges that the small yeti and the ban jhankri physically resemble one another (Conton 2001, 32). Further, among some learned Nepalese, their identity seems to be conventional wisdom. For example, a "cartoon funbook" written in English for tourists, and perhaps for Nepalese children learning English, describes yeti terminology. The Sherpa author Wangdi (1994, 23) lists the "local names" given to yeti, as follows:

Tibet = *metoh kangmi*

Bhutan = *migyu* (*me-göd*)

Sherpa = *ye-te, nalmu* (*nyalmo*)

Nepal = *ban manche, ban jhankri*

Tourist = *yeti*

(PARENTHESES MINE)

As has been demonstrated, the link between yeti and the ban jhankri is thematic as well as terminological. It is my hope that this book will rehabilitate interest in the study of the yeti as spirit teacher and initiator of shamans.

All researchers, past and current, attest that the Himalayan people unqualifiably believe in the O.R. existence of yeti. Still, it seems to me that shamans are aware of the N.O.R. quality of their abduction experiences. Many initiates, like Ram Ali, report that their encounter experience was dream-like; or that "paths" were opened for them that couldn't be perceived by others. Indeed, Gajendra used terms like "woke up" after an abduction ended, to indicate the return to his usual state of consciousness. He also maintained that the abductions were not the ordinary dreams of sleep. He was bodily abducted. That is to say, Gajendra was physically gone from home naked and in the forest until his parents finally found him three days later. They confirmed this. Som Maya, a shaman in Boudhanath, was abducted at seven years of age. She relates that her kin were already arranging her funeral when she was finally returned some days later by the ban jhankri (Eigner 2001, 25). Likewise, as discussed above, those who did not pass inspection maintained that they were similarly kidnapped and had disappeared from their villages for shorter periods, typically one day.

It is important to recognize that, to the ban jhankri initiates and to most Nepali, what occurs in dream and trance states are considered *real* experiences. Likewise, it is core to shamanism cross-culturally that "ordinary" and "nonordinary" are both "realities" (Harner 1990, 40, 44, 47, 53). To the ban jhankri shaman initiates, these realities overlap and are not conceptually separate from each other. That N.O.R.

experiences have effects in O.R. is a worldwide and essential belief in shamanic healing and ritual. The contents of an N.O.R. experience are not interpreted as symbolic of some underlying process (e.g., psychology). Rather, what is "seen" is taken at face value. Indeed, abduction experiences have an apparition-like quality, but this does not negate them as real happenings. Phenomenologically, they are what they *spontaneously* appear to be—real-time experiences. That is to say, they are N.O.R. encounters penetrating into the O.R. external world of perception. As said above, the existence of the ban jhankri or yeti is consensual reality in the culture. It is not only shamans and yogi who report seeing them and to have experienced them profoundly. However, only shamans develop relationship with them, are taught and initiated by them, and ultimately are, after training, able to access them voluntarily in ritual for purposes of community benefit.

Abduction experiences are not part of a community ritual, shamanic or otherwise. They are "spontaneous elections" in which spirit chooses the candidate; the election is a "spontaneous vocation" (Eliade 1964, 13, 109). Unlike definite "vision quests," shamanism is thrust upon the ban jhankri abductee. Often, abduction is preceded by an illness or by powerful dreams. When the ban jhankri comes and takes candidates, he is thought to *possess* them. Resistance is impossible. The veneer of cultural propriety vanishes. The novice runs wild and naked into the jungle and eats worms and tree bark with the back of his hands, wanders in cemeteries, sleeps in caves, and is beset with visions, his cultural expectations subjected to a wild destructuring. The ability to master such an experience is a tremendous accomplishment, especially for a child. Imagine how profound it would be if, for your entire young life, caretakers have told you, "Be good or the yeti will come and get you," and then, one night, they do! Those of pure heart must overcome fear and pay attention, learn, and acquire power from them.

REFERENCES

Aharon, Yonah N. ibn. "A Contribution to the Philology of ABSMery." In *Abominable Snowmen: Legend Comes to Life,* by Ivan Sanderson. Philadelphia: Chilton Company, 1961.

Anderson, Mary M. *The Festivals of Nepal.* Calcutta: Rupa and Company, 1975.

Bajracharya, Nunche B. *Swoyambu.* Kathmandu: Satyaho, 1985.

Basham, A. L. *The Wonder That Was India.* New York: Grove Press, Inc., 1954.

Berglie, Per-Arne. "Preliminary Remarks on Some Tibetan 'Spirit-Mediums' in Nepal." *Kailash: A Journal of Himalayan Studies* IV, no. 1 (1976): 85–108.

Bhairavan, Amarananda. *Kali's* Odiyya: *A Shaman's True Story of Initiation.* York Beach, ME: Nicholas-Hays, 2000.

Caldwell, Sarah. *Oh Terrifying Mother: Sexuality, Violence and Worship of the Goddess Kali.* New Delhi: Oxford University Press, 1999.

Chang, Garma C. C., translator and annotator. *The Hundred Thousand Songs of Milarepa.* Boston: Shambhala Publishing, 1962.

Choden, Kunzang. *Bhutanese Tales of the Yeti.* Bangkok: White Lotus Press, 1997.

Chophel, Norbu. *Folk Tales of Tibet.* Dharamsala, India: Library of Tibetan Works and Archives, 1984.

———. *Folk Culture of Tibet.* Dharamsala, India: Library of Tibetan Works and Archives, 1993.

Chorvinsky, Mark. "Yeti and the Cinema." In *Tom Slick and the Search for the Yeti,* edited by Loren Coleman. Boston: Faber and Faber, 1989.

Coleman, Loren. *Tom Slick and the Search for the Yeti.* Boston: Faber and Faber, 1989.

Conton, Leslie. "Encounters with Ban Jhankri: Shamanic Initiation by Abduction in Nepal." *Shamanism* 14, no. 2 (2001): 31–43.

Das, Sarat Chandra. *A Tibetan-English Dictionary.* Berkeley, CA: Shambhala Booksellers, 1974.

Desjarlais, Robert. "Healing through Images: The Magical Flight and Healing Geography of Nepali Shamans." *Ethos* 17, no. 3 (1989): 289–307.

———. *Body and Emotion: The Aesthetics of Illness and Healing in the Nepal Himalaya.* Philadelphia: University of Pennsylvania Press, 1992.

Dhakal, Shiva. *Folk Tales of Sherpa and Yeti.* New Delhi: Nirala, 1991.

Dietrich, Angela. *Tantric Healing in the Kathmandu Valley.* Delhi: Book Faith India, 1998.

Dowman, Keith. *The Power Places of Central Tibet: The Pilgrim's Guide.* London: Routledge & Kegan Paul, 1988.

Eigner, Dagmar. "Becoming a Shaman: Two Stories from Nepal." *Shamanism* 14, no. 2 (2001): 24–30.

Ekvall, Robert B. *Religious Observances in Tibet.* Chicago: University of Chicago Press, 1964.

———. *Fields of the Hoof: Nexus of Tibetan Nomadic Pastoralism.* New York: Holt, Rinehart and Winston, 1968.

Eliade, Mircea. *Yoga: Immortality and Freedom.* Princeton, NJ: Bollingen, Princeton University Press, 1958.

———. *Shamanism: Archaic Techniques of Ecstasy.* Princeton, NJ: Bollingen, Princeton University Press, 1964.

Evans-Wentz, W. Y. *Tibet's Great Yogi Milarepa: A Biography from the Tibetan.* London: Oxford University Press, 1951.

Fournier, Alain. "A Preliminary Report on the Puimbo and the Ngiami: The Sunuwar Shamans of Sabra." In *Spirit Possession in the Nepal Himalaya,* edited by John Hitchcock and Rex Jones. New Delhi: Vikas Publishing House Pvt. Ltd., 1976.

Fürer-Haimendorf, Christoph von. *The Sherpas of Nepal: Buddhist Highlanders.* New Delhi: Sterling Publishers Pvt. Ltd., 1964.

Gupta, Madan Mohan, and Tribhuvan Nath. *On the Yeti Trail: The Search for the Elusive Snowman.* New Delhi: Bombay Bangalore Madras Publishers, 1994.

Hagen, Toni. *Nepal: The Kingdom of the Himalaya.* Bern, Switzerland: Kümmerly & Frey, 1961.

Harner, Michael. *The Way of the Shaman.* San Francisco: HarperCollins, 1990.

Hillary, Edmund, and Desmond Doig. *High in the Thin Cold Air.* London: Hodder and Stoughton, 1962.

Hitchcock, John. "A Shaman's Song and Some Implications for the Himalayan Research." In *Contributions to the Anthropology of Nepal,* edited by Christoph von Fürer-Haimendorf, 150–158. Warminster, England: Aris & Phillips Ltd., 1974.

———. "Aspects of Bhujel Shamanism." In *Spirit Possession in the Nepal Himalaya,* edited by John Hitchcock and Rex Jones. New Delhi: Vikas Publishing House Pvt. Ltd., 1976.

Hoffmann, Helmut. *The Religions of Tibet.* Translated by Edward Fitzgerald. London: George Allen & Unwin Ltd., 1961.

Jäschke, H. A. *A Tibetan-English Dictionary.* London: Routledge & Kegan Paul Ltd., 1972.

Kohn, Richard J. *Lord of the Dance: The Mani Rimdu Festival in Tibet and Nepal.* Albany: State University of New York Press, 2001.

Krippner, Stanley, Fariba Bogzaran, and André Percia de Carvalho. "Called to Be Dreamers: Initiatory and Lucid Dreams." *Shaman's Drum* 61 (2002): 19–27.

Lall, Kesar. *Lore and Legend of the Yeti.* Kathmandu: Pilgrims Book House, 1988a.

———. *Tales of the Yeti.* Kathmandu: Pilgrims Book House, 1988b.

Li An-Che. "Bon: The Magico-Religious Belief of the Tibetan-Speaking Peoples." *Southwestern Journal of Anthropology* IV, no. 1 (1948): 31–41.

Macdonald, A. W. "Preliminary Notes on Some *Jhakri* of the Muglan." In *Spirit Possession in the Nepal Himalaya,* edited by John Hitchcock and Rex Jones. New Delhi: Vikas Publishing House Pvt. Ltd., 1976.

Majupuria, Trilok Chandra, and Rohit Kumar. *Yeti* (*The Abominable Snowman of the Silent Snows of the Himalaya*): *Fact or Fiction.* Lashkar, India: Smt. M. D. Gupta, 1993.

Maskarinec, Gregory. *The Rulings of the Night: An Ethnography of Nepalese Shaman Texts.* Madison: University of Wisconsin Press, 1995.

Messner, Reinhold. *My Quest for the Yeti.* Translated by Peter Constantine. New York: St. Martin's Press, 2000.

Miller, Casper. *Faith-Healers in the Himalaya.* Delhi: Book Faith India, 1997.

Mookerjee, Ajit. *Kali: The Feminine Force.* London: Thames & Hudson, 1988.

Mumford, Stan R. *Himalayan Dialogue: Tibetan Lamas and Gurung Shamans in Nepal.* Kathmandu: Tiwari's Pilgrims Book House, 1989.

Napier, John. *Bigfoot: The Yeti and Sasquatch in Myth and Reality.* New York: E. P. Dutton & Co., Inc., 1973.

Nebesky-Wojkowitz, René de. *Where the Gods Are Mountains.* Translated by Michael Bullock. New York: Reynal & Co., 1956.

———. *Oracles and Demons of Tibet.* Kathmandu: Tiwari's Pilgrims Book House, 1993 (originally published 1956).

Norbu, Thubten Jigme, and Colin Turnbull. *Tibet: Its History, Religion and People.* Middlesex, England: Penguin Books, 1972.

O'Flaherty, Wendy Doniger. *The Origins of Evil in Hindu Mythology.* Berkeley: University of California Press, 1976.

Oppitz, Michael. "Oral Traditions in Himalayan Shamanic Practice." In *Notes from the International Symposium on Discovery of Shamanic Heritage,* 137–156. Seoul: Korean National Commission for UNESCO, 1998.

Panday, Ramkumar. *Yeti Accounts.* Kathmandu: Ratna Pustak Bhandar, 1994.

Pattanaik, Devdutt. *Shiva: An Introduction.* Mumbai, India: Vakils, Feffer and Simons Ltd., 1977.

Paul, Robert. "Some Observations of Sherpa Shamanism." In *Spirit Possession in the Nepal Himalaya,* edited by John Hitchcock and Rex Jones. New Delhi: Vikas Publishing House Pvt. Ltd., 1976.

———. *The Tibetan Symbolic World.* Chicago: University of Chicago Press, 1982.

Peters, Larry. "Concepts of Mental Deficiency among the Tamang of Nepal." *American Journal of Mental Deficiency* 84, no. 4 (1980): 352–356.

———. *Ecstasy and Healing in Nepal: An Ethnopsychiatric Study of Tamang Shamanism.* Los Angeles: Undena Press, 1981. Revised edition, retitled *Tamang Shamans.* New Delhi: Nirala, 1998.

———. "Trance, Initiation, and Psychotherapy in Tamang Shamanism." *American Ethnologist* 91 (1982): 21–36.

———. "Shamanism: Phenomenology of a Spiritual Discipline." *The Journal of Transpersonal Psychology* (1989): 115–137.

———. "*Karga Puja:* A Transpersonal Ritual of Healing in Tamang Shamanism." *Alternative Therapies in Health and Medicine* 1, no. 5 (1995): 53–61.

———. "The 'Calling,' the Yeti, and the Ban Jhakri ('Forest Shaman') in Nepalese Shamanism." *The Journal of Transpersonal Psychology* 29, no. 1 (1997a): 47–62.

———. "The Tibetan Healing Rituals of Dorje Yüdronma: A Fierce Manifestation of Feminine Cosmic Force." *Shaman's Drum* 45 (1997b): 37–48.

———. "Some Elements of the Shamanism of Pau Wang Chuk." *Shamanism: Journal of the Foundation for Shamanic Studies* 10, no. 2 (1997c): 21–23.

———. *Tamang Shamans: An Ethnopsychiatric Study of Ecstasy and Healing in Nepal.* New Delhi: Nirala Publications, 1999.

———. "The *Man Chinni* Exorcism Rite of Tamang Shamans." *Shaman's Drum* 55 (2000): 17–25.

———. *Trance, Initiation, and Psychotherapy in Nepalese Shamanism: Essays on Tamang and Tibetan Shamanism.* New Delhi: Nirala Publications, 2004.

Peters, Larry, and Douglass Price-Williams. "Towards an Experiential Analysis of Shamanism." *American Ethnologist* 7, no. 2 (1980): 397–448.

———. "A Phenomenological Overview of Trance." *Transcultural Psychiatric Research Review* 20, no. 1 (1983): 5–39.

Pravananda, Swami. "Abominable Snowman." *The Indian Geographical Journal* 30, no. 3 (1955): 99–104.

Riboli, Diana. *Tunsuriban: Shamanism in the Chepang of Southern and Central Nepal.* Kathmandu: Mandala Book Point, 2000.

Sagant, Phillippe. "Becoming a Limbu Priest." In *Spirit Possession in the*

Nepal Himalaya, edited by John Hitchcock and Rex Jones. New Delhi: Vikas Publishing House Pvt. Ltd., 1976.

Samuel, Geoffrey. *Civilized Shamans: Buddhism in Tibetan Societies.* Washington, DC: Smithsonian Institution Press, 1993.

Sanderson, Ivan T. *Abominable Snowmen: Legend Comes to Life.* Philadelphia: Chilton Company, 1961.

Saunders, Nicholas J. *Animal Spirits.* Boston: Little, Brown and Company, 1995.

Schuhmacher, Stephan, and Gert Woerner, eds. *The Encyclopedia of Eastern Philosophy and Religion.* Boston: Shambhala Press, 1989.

Shackley, Myra. *Still Living? Yeti, Sasquatch and the Neanderthal Enigma.* New York: Thames & Hudson, Inc., 1983.

Shakabpa, Tsepon W. D. *Tibet: A Political History.* New Haven, CT: Yale University Press, 1967.

Sharma, Nagendra. *Folk Tales of Nepal.* New Delhi: Learners Press Pvt. Ltd., 1996.

Sifers, Sarah, and Larry G. Peters. "Pau Wangchuk: Status Report of FSS' First 'Living Treasure.'" *Shamanism: Journal of the Foundation for Shamanic Studies* 14 (2001): 31–34.

Skafte, Peter. "Three Accounts of Shamanic Initiation from Nepal." *Shaman's Drum* 27 (1992): 46–52.

Slusser, Mary. *Nepal Mandala: A Cultural Study of the Kathmandu Valley, Volume 1: Text.* Princeton, NJ: Princeton University Press, 1998.

Snellgrove, David L. *Buddhist Himalaya.* Oxford: Bruno Cassirer, 1957.

Spindler, George, and Louise Spindler. "Foreword." In *Fields on the Hoof: Nexus of Tibetan Nomadic Pastoralism,* edited by Robert Ekvall. New York: Holt, Rinehart and Winston, 1968.

Stein, R. A. *Tibetan Civilization.* Translated by J. E. Stapleton Driver. Stanford, CA: Stanford University Press, 1972.

Strasenburgh, Gordon. "Book Review: *North America's Great Ape: The Sasquatch,* by John A. Bendernagel." *Journal of Scientific Exploration* 13, no. 2 (1999): 549–552.

Tucci, Giuseppe. *The Theory and Practice of the Mandala.* Translated by A. H. Broderick. New York: Samuel Weiser, 1961.

———. *The Religions of Tibet.* Translated by Geoffrey Samuel. Berkeley: University of California Press, 1988 (originally published 1970).

Waddell, L. Austine. *The Buddhism of Tibet or Lamaism,* 3rd ed. Cambridge, England: W. Heffer & Sons, Ltd., 1971.

Wangdi, Gyamcho. *Mysterious Mystical Yeti.* Kathmandu: Modern Printing Press, 1994.

Zimmer, Heinrich. *Myths and Symbols in Indian Art and Civilization.* Princeton, NJ: Princeton University Press, 1972.

GLOSSARY OF FOREIGN TERMS

(Bh)	= Bhutanese	(S)	= Sanskrit
(L)	= Lepcha	(Sh)	= Sherpa
(M)	= Mongolian	(T)	= Tibetan
(N)	= Nepali	(Ta)	= Tamang

almas (M)	large cattle eater, or a small (five- to six-foot) wildman
aph se aph (N)	spontaneously arising out of itself, self-generated
ban devi (N)	forest goddess
ban jhankri (N)	forest shaman
ban jhankrini (N)	female forest shaman
ban kali (N)	forest Kali
ban manche (N)	forest man, connoting a wild nature
banpa (N)	forest spirits

Böd (T)	people of Tibet
bodhisattva (S)	enlightened one, in Buddhism
boksha (N)	sorcerer/witch
bokshi (N)	female sorcerer/witch
bombo (T, Sh)	shaman
Bönpo (T)	shamanic pre-Buddhist spirituality of Tibet
che-mo (T)	female bear
chokho (N)	pure, sacred
chom (Sh)	bear
chu-mung (L)	spirit of the glaciers
chut-te (T, Sh)	water *yeti*
dhankini (N)	spirit sorceress
dharma (S)	Buddhist teachings
dharmapala (S)	Buddhist demigod protectors of the faith
dre (*de*) (T)	bear or demon
dred-mo (T)	female bear
dzu-te (T)	large, strong, aggressive cattle eater
gang-mi (Sh)	glacier man
gemaka (Sh)	killer spirits
göd (T)	untamed, wild
jangali admi (N)	wildman of the woods (jungle man)
jhankri (N)	shaman
jutho (N)	spiritual pollution

juti (Sh)	large, strong, aggressive cattle eater
kangme (T)	snowman
laato (N)	dumb, slow, simple person
lüd (T)	scapegoat
man (N)	heart-mind
mantra (S)	sacred syllables
me (T)	man
me-chen-po (T)	great man
me-göd (T)	wildman, often spelled *mi-gyu,* small *yeti*
me-te (T, Sh)	*yeti,* bear-man/thing of diminutive size
mi-bom-po (Sh)	(wild) man shaman
mi-dre (Sh)	man-demon
mi-gyu (T, Bh)	ape-man
mutu (N)	heart organ
nyalbu (T)	bastard child of a whore
nyalmo (T)	female *yeti;* also a semihuman, fierce, sexually aggressive, large mountain demoness
nyalpa (*ba*) (T)	coitus
phurba (T)	magical dagger
raksas (S)	demon
rang shi (T)	spontaneous manifestation
rang shi bombo/ bompo (T)	self-generated shaman, small *yeti, ban jhankri*
rang shi tugpa (Ta)	self-generated without effort, automatically

ri-bombo (Sh)	mountain shaman, *ban jhankri*
ri mi (T, Sh)	mountain man, midsize *yeti*
rinpoché (T)	learned incarnate *lama;* literally "precious gem"
shen (T)	Bönpo sacrificial priest
sikhari (N)	hunter spirits
sin-mo (T)	fierce mountain goddesses of the pre-Buddhist Bön faith of Tibet
sogpa (*sokpa*) (T)	giant demon that looks like an ape
sunna (N)	golden
te (*toh*) (T)	bear
teh-ima (T)	man-like thing/bear
terma (T)	discovered or revealed sacred text, authorship attributed to Padma Sambhava
thangka (T)	painted scroll used as an aid in meditation
thom (Sh)	bear
ti (N)	third-person pronoun at a distance (those)
torma (T)	barley flour effigies
tre (T)	bear
tse (T)	life or living thing
ulto-sulto (N)	right way/opposite or contrary way
ya (*yeh*) (Sh)	cliff dweller
yaksa (S)	Hindu and Buddhist demigod
yaksi or *yakshini* (S)	fierce Hindu-Buddhist demigoddess
ye (*yi*) (N)	third-person pronoun (these)

·6·

THE GHE-WA (TIBETAN DEATH RITE) *for* PAU KARMA WANGCHUK NAMGYAL

The early morning March sun and clear skies warmed the streets at Lakeside in Pokhara, Nepal, and offered a fine view of the white-capped Machapuchare or "Fishtail" mountain. The towering Himalayas are an awesome presence and are themselves considered to be deities. On clear days, they dominate the landscape. I had just arrived in Pokhara, and was walking to the home of Yeshi Gyatso and Migmar Choezam, husband and wife, wonderful friends whom I have known and worked with for more than a decade. Migmar is an expert Tibetan translator and always a great help in accessing the Tibetan shamans residing outside Pokhara at the refugee camp that H. H. the Dalai Lama named Tashi Palkhiel (Tibetan for "auspicious blooming"). The eldest of these shamans (pau) was Karma Wangchuk (see Figure 6-1).

The streets of Pokhara's Lakeside bazaar were quiet that morning. Perhaps it was too early for the many tourists who have flocked to Pokhara this year. Some of the shops had just opened, and the street vendors were laying out their handicrafts on blankets. One of them recognized me and we spoke. "*Tashi deleg,*" she greeted me in Tibetan. "When did you return? Have you heard about Wangchuk?" I had been coming to Pokhara to meet with Wangchuk and the other pau for three or four days a few times a year since 1994. I had seen many of his healings and heard many stories. And, on the streets that day, I heard some of these stories again: about the day a young boy who had swallowed a coin and was near death when Wangchuk, embodied by the "deities radiant," extracted the coin from the boy's throat using a hollow ram's horn, saving his life; or about the man who had swallowed a fish bone that had festered for days before Wangchuk extracted it, now greatly enlarged, bloody, and filled with pus.[51]

One day, I saw Wangchuk do a divination for a colleague, David H., who, like me, is a student of Michael Harner and Core Shamanism, and had come to Nepal to learn and be initiated. It was probably the most powerful divination rite I had ever witnessed. Wangchuk played his dharu, a small, two-sided hand drum, then laid it flat on the small table in front of the bed from which he worked. Now Wangchuk scattered some white rice on the drum, sat back, said some mantra, and blew toward the drum. I watched as most grains of rice began to bounce and then turn counterclockwise, following each other in a circle around the periphery of the drum skin. Meanwhile, many of the grains were spinning clockwise on their own axis. It was an amazing spectacle, but even more amazing was the divination that followed, i.e., what Wangchuk saw in the dancing rice. Something like, "There is an accident back home; you should make contact."

Indeed, there had been an auto accident back home, a door unhinged by a passing car that nearly missed David's wife and baby, as I recall. But all was okay; no one was hurt, as Wangchuk had accurately divined. Later I discovered the clockwise turning of the rice on its axis indicated a favorable result.

Then there was Judy W., another Foundation student who has since passed on. I received a card from her some years ago with a picture of Wangchuk performing a healing on her. The inside of the card read: "When I went to Nepal, I was sick with hepatitis-like symptoms. Here Wangchuk, a traditional Tibetan shaman in a Tibetan refugee camp outside Pokhara, Nepal, extracts a piece of porous bone from my chest. He removed it through his damaru (drum) and a very curly ram's horn. The symptoms went away and subsequent blood tests back home showed all normal levels. He did indicate that there were more serious problems. Love, Judy. December 2001." Less than two years later, bone cancer caused Judy's death. Her presence alongside Wangchuk is a vivid memory.

During all the years I came to visit with Wangchuk, he was frail, about five feet tall, and thin (perhaps ninety pounds). He had bouts with tuberculosis and had trouble breathing, falling victim more than once to pneumonia, and requiring a small respirator before and after his rituals. Yet, he vigorously played his dharu (small drum) in his right hand, and his shang (hand bell) in his left, jumping to his feet to dance, dressed in full regalia, with a ringa (crown) of the five Wisdom (dhyana) Buddhas with broad, flapping rainbow wings on either side.

He was a gentle soul and I will always remember him in the camp's center, smiling while turning a very large prayer wheel, and wearing around his neck dozens of the white conch cylinders strung together that he had worn out from the perpetual turning. There was a lot of tragedy in Wangchuk's life. Driven from his homeland by the Chinese invasion, he came to Nepal with only what he could carry on his back. His wife, Tsering, is very withdrawn and rarely coherent, a condition that has worsened over the years. His elder son, who had served as the "mediator" assisting Wangchuk during shamanic healing rituals, died from alcoholism and from having drunk poison. Some in the community blamed Wangchuk, a backbiting I found very sad. At the time, I thought it must be common parlance, because they were telling me, a virtual stranger. Despite all this hardship, Wangchuk's shamanic work remained undaunted.

Wangchuk deeply missed his Tibetan homeland and spoke fondly of the nomadic way of life, expeditions to obtain salt from the north requiring a few hundred kilometers' walk while herding the cattle (yak and the female do). He had a critical mind and wit, and told others in the camp that, if they were to return to Tibet, they would not know how to survive. Laughing, he'd say they would freeze, because it was so cold in Tibet that "rocks would break." Migmar also told me that he said, "When a bird dies, it thinks of its nest; when a person dies, he thinks of his home (i.e., homeland)."

THE PSYCHOPOMPIC RITE GIVEN FOR WANGCHUK

The forty-ninth day after death is the final day of the ghe-wa, an extraordinary psychopompic event. That day, numerous members of the camp came to give honor to Wangchuk. The shaman Sri-chöd came, as did the other shaman in the camp, Nyima. Nyima's brother and shamanic mediator, Karma Tsedup, was there for the entire ritual and was a big participant. Karma, along with ten men from the camp, sat around a large metal container and, with bare hands, kneaded a mixture of mostly tsampa (roasted barley flour), molasses, and milk to form many small, cone-shaped sweet delicacies to be distributed to all who came to the ghe-wa, along with cookies, chips, rolls, bags of candy, cheese puffs, etc. (see Figure 6-2). This practice is called *tshog*. Food was also given to Wangchuk's family by members of the community. Eventually, representatives from the camp came and took large plastic bags full of goodies back to their areas. As I helped fill the bags, I was thinking that there wouldn't be one person in the perhaps 1,400-person camp who wouldn't get at least one bag of goodies from Wangchuk's funeral.

Wangchuk died at about 5:30 p.m. on January 25, 2008, at the age of eighty-eight. Tilley, his youngest son, had brought him some tea and noticed he was not breathing. The lama Rabten Rinpoche, from the Jang Chub Choeling Gompa in the camp, was called in to test the pulse and breath. One of the monks, Sonam Rinchen, was asked to divine through astrology what should happen to the body, whether Wangchuk should be buried, burned, or cut up and given to the birds, fish, and other animals; as well as how long to wait before any of this should occur.

At this time, Rabten Rinpoche did a *pho-wa,* a rite in which the hair is pulled on the corpse, in order to open the top of the head. It is believed to be effective if a drop of blood appears on the very top of the scalp. Yeshi and Migmar, my translators and teachers who provided much of the information below, explained that pho-wa makes the "skull as soft as that of an infant" so that the soul (nam-shé) can pass easily from the body. After this, a white scarf (khatak) is wrapped around the neck so as to prohibit the soul from reentering and/or another spirit from reanimating the body.

I was told that many butter lamps were lit and placed at the top of the bed where Wangchuk had died and now lay, in order to send him good wishes, to light the way, and to help remove any obstacles that might interfere with his soul's journey through the bardo, that intermediary state between death and rebirth, as taught in the *Bardo Thodol.*[52]

If possible, it is customary that a thangka (a colorful, painted sacred scroll framed in embroidered silk) of a specific deity, and a statue of a deity, are placed on or near the altar in the room of the ghe-wa. The lama had previously divined that the deity Amitabha,[53] the red Buddha, should adorn the thangka and that the statue should be of Manjusri, an enlightened sage and Buddha of a former age.

Thanks to the generosity of Michael Harner and the Foundation for Shamanic Studies, its members, field representatives, and others, these items were secured and had a prominent position and function during the rite.

Sonam Rinchen, the monk and astrologer, instructed that the body be removed from the house at 3:00 a.m. and taken to the newly constructed *ghat,* a place where Wangchuk's body was burned at the edge of the White River (Seti Khola) below the camp. The ghat was consecrated by many lama; at its bottom is a mandala that is a potent help to send the soul into the bardo, even if a pho-wa had not been performed, Yeshi maintained. The fire ceremony (*ginzag*) was performed by Rabten Rinpoche, and attended by twenty monks. After the body was burned, the remaining bones were collected and kept for the following forty-nine-day rite. The ashes were swept into the river.

It is written in the commentaries to *The Tibetan Book of the Dead,* which guides the soul or consciousness and the lama's work during the ghe-wa for forty-nine days, that the text also has a profound effect on the living. In fact, from my perspective, Wangchuk's ghe-wa was a great healing for the kin left behind.

Wangchuk's daughter Dolma, son-in-law Dawa, and their two children came from India to attend the ghe-wa rite. Wangchuk had only recently been reunited with them, after years of estrangement. Migmar said he was quite happy for the last year of his life. When they came for the ghe-wa, they went to Wangchuk's son Tilley's wife's parents' house and brought her back, as she had been separated from him. Further, they expressed care and concern about Tilley's future, as jobs are few and the economy in the camp, and around Nepal, is very weak. It was obvious that Wangchuk's death would have dire financial consequences for the entire family.

For forty-nine days, there was supposed to be a butter lamp burning twenty-four hours each day. It is the family's responsibility to ensure this occurs. I observed that this was so on the days I was there, up to the end of the ghe-wa on March 14.

On the third day after death, it is said that the deceased "wakes up" and has "clear thinking," even more so than before death. He is surprised to see others sad and tries to "sit with them," and speak, but to no avail. He looks around and sees the offerings, the lamps, and the food, his favorites left for him. Then the thought occurs that he "may be dead." And he tests to see if he "leaves footprints,"[54] sees his "image in a mirror," or "gets through a small hole." Then he realizes that he is dead and is sad, and dies for a "second time" on that third day. That is to say, his spirit comes to the realization of having died and this perception is traumatic. The family is implored not to cry, for the spirit of the deceased is already in much pain that will likely increase if he sees them in tears. The above account was given by Yeshi and Migmar, and from an interview with Karma Tsedup.

On this important day, the family did a ritual called *sur,* which was repeated each day from the third to the forty-ninth day. In sur, tsampa is mixed with sugar and burned as a fire offering, and five things are gathered for the five senses: music from a bell; juniper incense to smell; a mirror; the deceased's favorite food is prepared; and a red and white cloth for touch. Tilley told me Wangchuk was left a cup of milk tea with each meal offering, as was his habit in life. All of these offerings are made at precise times, three times for each of the days following death, as the spirit will likely be near his home and kin, so it is important to make these offerings for the deceased's happiness while the spirit is close.

On days four, five, six, and seven, the lama return to read from the *Book of the Dead* in order to guide the soul through the bardo, reminding it to merge with the great lights of the Wisdom Buddhas; that is, to take refuge in them. Special attention is given to the red Buddha Amitabha on the seventh day, as the lama speak directly to Wangchuk's soul about this Buddha, who is depicted on the thangka, reminding the soul to take refuge there. Migmar explained that all Tibetans desire to take refuge in Amitabha, who is the spiritual father of Chenrezig, the patron saint of Tibet, the Bodhisattva of Compassion, and is incarnated in each successive Dalai Lama.

Essentially this structure is maintained for all seven weeks, thus totaling forty-nine days. The middle of the fourth week after death, and the forty-ninth day, are very important days for the destiny of the soul. These two days have a similar structure and elements. According to Yeshi and Migmar, those are the days on which the bardo journey comes to an end. That is, the soul may be fortunate enough to complete its journey in half the time, due to good karma. Still, there is no guarantee, and thus all forty-nine days of the rite must be completed. Sonam Rinchen had divined that Wangchuk's soul would be reborn to a household with three brothers. This was all that was said, but questions about the direction of the village and other circumstances of the rebirth may be foretold as well.

On these two important days, there are a number of remarkable aspects. The following account is from my notes on the forty-ninth day, as I was not there to attend at the midpoint. There was much discussion among the participants of what happened on the day of Wangchuk's death. There was an electrical blackout for hours, and Wangchuk may have needed his respirator. He had completed his work but instead of putting away his costume and ritual instruments, he left them out, which he had not done before. They were left unwrapped and not in his bag. Many who attended thought this indicated he had died almost immediately after completing a ritual. I had the opportunity, along with Tilley, to prostrate myself to his gear, which had been left exactly where Wangchuk left it. We also prostrated ourselves in front of the Amitabha thangka, and hung a silk greeting scarf (khatak) around the thangka and the Manjusri statue. We also bowed to the collection of Wangchuk's bones, some of which were mixed with his ashes and clay to form a mushroom-like structure called a *tsa tsa,* which would be left by Tilley at the holy shrine of Muktinath, about a five-day walk, and at an altitude of 12,500 feet, after the ceremony. Also prominent in the room that day, as it had been on most days Wangchuk was doing his healing work, was a thangka of Thang Lha, one of Wangchuk's most important spirits, which had been presented to him years before by Sarah Sifers, a field associate of the Foundation like myself. On the thangka, Thang Lha is depicted in his peaceful form, seated upon a white horse. Thang Lha is also the name of a large mountain range in south-central Tibet as well as a pre-Buddhist deity of the nomadic Tibetan shamans who, it is told, was converted to Buddhism by Padma Sambhava himself.[55]

Accompanied by the dramatic, transic musical mélange of cymbals, large hanging drums, resonant long horns, and intermittent chanting, Nyedon Rinpoche, the lama from the large nearby monastery who conducted the ghe-wa from the third day forward, took a *jangpur,* which is a piece of paper with Tibetan prayers, mantra, and the name Wangchuk written upon it, and then attached a photograph of Wangchuk (see Figure 6-3). The paper was fastened to a metal, cross-like structure, then burned, and the ashes collected in a bronze plate while the "waters of rebirth" were poured on them from a golden bum pa, the auspicious "vessel of treasure" for great blessings. At the same time, and with the same hand with which the Rinpoche held the vessel, he also held a brass mirror (ling). Thus, when the picture and paper were in flames, the mirror was directly opposite and reflecting the fire. And, when the water was poured into the plate, the mirror tilted down toward the blackened paper. Yeshi explained that the water in the bum pa was like the "endless river of long life ... with all the benefits of liberation."

As explained to me later by the shaman Nyima, the Rinpoche had called Wangchuk's soul into the mirror first, and then, when the soul sees its image being burned, it breaks all attachments to its current life and is reborn. Sitting in the little, one-room house where Wangchuk had conducted so many healings, watching his ghe-wa, I experienced a vivid memory of seeing a huge, white kite with a golden beak perched outside the window while he worked. This had been a common occurrence on most of the days I visited with Wangchuk. When I took a break and stepped outside, I noticed the bird circling not far from the house.

At nightfall, just before the ceremony ended, I read Michael Harner's letter of condolence honoring Wangchuk to the family (see page 174). Migmar translated word for word. It touched everyone, and I was very happy to have had that responsibility.

FINAL REMARKS

The ghe-wa of Wangchuk psychopomped his soul through all the phases of the bardo between death and rebirth as mentioned in the Tibetan text (see Figure 6-4). At the moment of death, the text describes, one finds oneself in the Chikhai Bardo of the Great White Light. Soon thereafter, it is said that, for those great rinpoché who have attained enlightenment, a rainbow light surrounds the body of the deceased and takes it directly to heaven, leaving no physical trace behind. If the White Light bardo is missed, the soul has the opportunity of having a vision of the Wisdom Buddhas of the five lights (yellow, white, red, green, and blue) of the Chönyid Bardo, the second bardo condition. These are the very Buddhas portrayed on the crown (ringa) worn by Wangchuk.

By now, the soul has become aware of its death. The lama and monks recite instructions to the soul not to merge with the lesser lights of mundane desires but to see the great lights of the five rainbow colors and take refuge with the Buddhas therein. It is important that the soul recognize that obstacles of fear, wanting, and anger may arise in the form of frightening images. However, the soul is instructed to recognize these images as no other than aspects of oneself. And what appears to be frightening is really good inside, I was told.

If the soul retains that clear, mirror-like consciousness and overcomes these obstacles, it can take refuge with the Buddhas and Bodhisattvas who have renounced *nirvana* in order to help us humans in the bardo between death and birth as well as between birth and death.

The Tibetan Book of the Dead now turns to the Sidpa Bardo, the third bardo condition, and gives instructions for the souls of those who missed the opportunity to take refuge in the Buddhas of the second bardo. The Sidpa Bardo is the condition just prior to incarnation in which the soul is drawn by impulse to its future mother's womb and reborn according to its karma. This could be in any of six worlds. The most fortunate is the human world, the realm into which Wangchuk has again been born.

The Tibetan Book of the Dead and the ghe-wa I attended for Wangchuk both seem to teach that consciousness (or soul) is eternal. Its destiny is set upon a great wheel, symbol of the endless cycle from birth to rebirth, over and over again, until liberation is found from the obstacles we carry in heart and mind.

Such a psychologically sophisticated spiritual system, which is fundamental to the ghe-wa, resonates in the culture of the Tibetan people at the camp. Wangchuk's ghe-wa had a deep effect on me. The eight days I spent playing, visiting, and learning in the camp are impossible to describe. There was much heart in that rite and from the people at the camp, and in the monks' ritual chanting at the ghe-wa and in the camp monastery rituals every morning and evening. Each day, so many gave so much love, even while they were suffering from their loss. In that camp, there is a slice of heaven, an auspicious blooming, a Tashi Palkhiel.

February 14, 2008

Dear Family of the Esteemed Pau Wangchuk,

On behalf of the Foundation for Shamanic Studies, I wish to extend my condolences on the passing of this great shaman. Despite all ordeals and difficulties, he made a great contribution by preserving and applying the ancient knowledge and powers of Tibetan shamanism to alleviate suffering and spiritual ignorance. His work also demonstrated to the world that this most ancient part of Tibetan spiritual culture was alive and worthy of respect and value.

Pau Wangchuk was one of a small number of shamans recognized internationally by the Foundation as a Living Treasure of Shamanism. It was an honor to help support him and his work, and it is also an honor to remember him and his life of compassionate partnership with the spirits as he generously helped others cope with the difficulties of human existence. He remains an inspiration for those throughout the world who are also struggling to preserve and revive shamanic knowledge and practice.

His material body may be gone, but his example lives. I send my prayers for him and his family as he moves beyond ordinary human life.

With my greatest respect and best wishes,

—*Michael Harner*

ENDNOTES

1 All foreign terms are Tibetan unless otherwise indicated.

2 All foreign terms are in Tibetan unless otherwise indicated. Whenever possible, I have used the phonetic spoken by the shamans interviewed. The transliteration from written Tibetan is given in brackets where a key term is first used if different from the phonetic. The foreign terms will facilitate future research and the research presented here subject to validation. Fieldwork was conducted with the aid of Migmar Choezam, my translator for almost twelve years. My language training is in classical Tibetan. I do not speak any of the Tibetan dialects. I wish to thank Michael Harner for his continuing moral support of my research into shamanism.

3 *Pahmo* [*dpah mo*] and *pahwo* or pau [*dpah bo*] are the terms referring to female and male "spirit mediums," respectively. The literal meaning is a "brave" or "courageous" woman or man. *Lhapa* (god man) and *lhamo* (god woman) are terms used for the same type of spirit medium, but those at the camp typically refer to themselves as pau. Tibetan "spirit mediumship" meets the cross-cultural criteria for "shamanic trance" developed by Eliade (1964) and Harner (1990).

4 The transliteration from Tibetan script is Sri Gcöd; he is also known as Pasang (because he was born on Friday), Rhichoe, Sri Choe, and Se Chur, the latter three being different attempts at pronunciation of Sri Gcöd. When speaking of himself, he says See Ché, as I hear it. Be this as it may, *sri* are death-causing spirits in a family, especially of children; *gcöd* means "to cut off." *Sri gcöd* is the name of the ritual to sever the hold of the sri. The shaman had this ritual and was given the name as an infant. I am herein employing the name Rhichoe for consistency with other publications and literature of the FSS.

[5] The word Bön is etymologically related to Böd, the term for Tibet in the Tibetan language (Tucci 1988, 213).

[6] *Lama* are priests (Jäschke 1972, 383) or *guru* (Tucci 1988, 44). Lama is a title generally used to politely identify almost any red-robed Tibetan male adult. Lama is not an official rank nor is it indicative of ritual status. In this book, Lamaism means the Buddhism of Tibet, and lama means its priests.

[7] According to Pau Nyima, pau do not eat nettles. They are a taboo food for pau except one day a year to honor Milarepa.

[8] The end result of the story varies among different Tibetan populations, depending on the extent of Buddhist influence. The protagonist in some versions is Padma Sambhava and not Milarepa (Hoffmann 1961, 25, 99; Peters 1998, 58).

[9] Lhamo Dolkar, a female Tibetan shaman who resided in Boudhanath near Kathmandu, received a similar letter from H. H. the Dalai Lama sanctioning her work after she was called to Dharamsala for healings (Peters 1997b, 38, 47).

[10] Jib is practiced only by pau and it is by far the most frequent type of ritual remedy.

[11] Shortened form of the Sanskrit *dhamaru.*

[12] Tshé is a more formal rendition of saug according to my translator Migmar, and is the term found in Buddhist literature (cf. Das 1974, 1029).

[13] Khatak are also known as "ceremonial scarves" or "salutation scarves" and are ubiquitously given by Tibetans as a way to honor a person, express gratitude, and greet guests or dignitaries (Das 1974, 128; Nebesky-Wojkowitz 1955, 206). Woven into the silk fabric, on the vast majority of these scarves, are the eight auspicious Buddhist signs of good fortune.

[14] According to Ermakov (2008, 524) and Stein (1972, 226), the Bön term for soul loss is *bla hkhyams pa.* For the camp pau, *la kyem pa* [bla hkhyams pa] or the roaming about of the la soul happens only at death when the la abandons the body. At this point, the la becomes a *shee dré* [*çi dre*] or ghost, and may roam about unless the proper funeral ceremony is performed by lama.

15 In the first method of la kuk described above, the slingshotting of the spag sheep image, which, except for a few particles, is not retrieved with the stones, may well be a survival or remnant functionally analogous to the "ransoming the soul" for the sheep's leg. If so, such a meaning has been lost to history.

16 Thang Lha (see Figure 1-7) is the ruling deity of the Nyan Chen Thang Lha mountain range, which stretches for hundreds of miles through northern Tibet and is said to have 360 peaks. Thang Lha, its personification, has 360 helpers in his entourage. Thang Lha is a dharmapala or sung mo and is the protector deity of the hill on which the Potala (H. H. the Dalai Lama's residence and seat of government in Lhasa) is built. He was converted to Buddhism by Padma Sambhava himself. His appearance can be benign, but some of the work he does is reserved for wrathful deities. He is known as the "executioner of all oath breakers" and of "all spirits that refuse to be converted to dharmapala." His residence is high in the snow-capped mountains, in the glaciers, and in the atmosphere between the sky and earth. He is called the "great *nyan* [*gnyan chen*]" and rides a flying white horse. The nyan are middle world deities usually associated with mountains, but also with fire, wind, and water. In Figure 1-7 Nyan Chen Thang Lha carries a victory flag in one hand and, in the other, the small rounded objects are Buddhist "precious jewels" (*nor bu*) whose lights of various colors radiate and, wherever present, there is no sickness and the mind is in equanimity (Nebesky-Wojkowitz 1993, 208f.; Rinpoche 1995, 70–71). Nyima's chief deity Thang Lha was also the chief deity for Wangchuk, and they channeled Thang Lha at almost every ritual of theirs I attended.

17 This description is specific to the pau's method of refuge. However, in the Lamaist tradition, refuge also involves the deities' light being absorbed into the practitioner (Beyer 1973, 437). This is quite distinct from the layperson's understanding of refuge and from the contexts in which the word is commonly employed. In other words, there is a technical shamanic meaning that relates to the medium's trance that is distinct from the ordinary meaning of "taking refuge" given at the end of the last section.

18 Most of this description of the tsa comes from interviews with Thang Lha; that is, from Nyima while embodied. The method of conducting trance interviews with the spirit mediums was developed by Berglie (1976, 88, 93).

19 Some dharmapala have been elevated to heavenly god status and some others are said to be on their way (Nebesky-Wojkowitz 1993, 3ff.). The ferocious deity Nag Chen Po (the great black one) depicted on the altar second from right has achieved such elevation. Thang Lha has nearly achieved lha status and Pe Har too, the dharmapala embodied by the State Oracle (Né Jung [Gnas Cung]) depicted to the far right on the altar.

20 A similar ritual initiatory method involving the tying of the fourth fingers of each hand is employed in the training of Tibetan oracles (*chos skyong*) (Nebesky-Wojkowitz 1993, 417).

21 Again, la and nam shé (consciousness) are used interchangeably by the pau. However, in this context, they typically used the Buddhist term nam shé.

22 There are similar initiations for the shamans among the Tamang of Nepal, a Tibetan ethnic group, called *gufa* (cave) in Nepali (Peters 1982, 1990, 1998).

23 The chakra system of centers of subtle energy had its highest development on the subcontinent in Hindu Tantrism and thereby made its way into Tibetan Buddhism, influencing Tibetan shamanism (Eliade 1969, 319), albeit some groundwork for the assimilation into Bön of Tantric ideas might be pre-Buddhist (Stein 1972, 223–225). The origins of the belief in chakra-like systems, however, are obscure and very ancient. For example, something very similar appears in South Africa among !Kung shamans (see Katz 1973).

24 All foreign terms are in the phonetic Tibetan spoken by the shamans unless otherwise indicated. A generally accepted transliteration of the Tibetan terms is given in the glossary of Chapter 1.

25 Shamans are also known as *lhapa* (god man) and female shamans as *lhamo* (goddess). At the camp, *pau* is customary.

26 I am using the term "Nepali patients" to refer primarily to members of various groups who are of Tibetan ethnicity but are citizens of Nepal,

residents of Nepal from the time of recorded history, mostly Buddhist, and the largest segment of the population of Nepal. These groups include the Gurung, Magar, Tamang, Sherpa, Thakali, etc., and are culturally distinct from the recent Tibetan exiled immigrants who reside in the refugee camp.

27 Both *mala* and *mantra* are Nepali and Indian terms regularly spoken by the pau. There are many other loan-words. Most camp residents are bilingual, also speaking Nepali. Many are involved in commerce and therefore speak the lingua franca of Nepal. Those who sell goods in the tourist section of Pokhara also speak English with various degrees of competence.

28 *Shakti* is another commonly spoken loan-word.

29 *Saug* (or *sok*) is another name for the life soul. *Tshe* is used more commonly by the pau.

30 The term "embodiment" in reference to shamanic practice is preferable to "possession," which sometimes carries the inaccurate connotation of a psychopathology.

31 *Sutra* is another Nepali and Indian loan-word.

32 Foreign terms are Tibetan. Spelling is phonetic.

33 The views about the bardo are those of the shamans and laypeople.

34 See Chapter 6 for a description of the ghe-wa death rite.

35 Sarah Sifers's 2008 film depicts the shed phud ceremony being performed by Pau Nyima.

36 Dharmapala in Sanskrit.

37 For a more complete description, see Chapter 1.

38 I believe this is a symptom of the shamans' declining status at the refugee camp (see Chapter 1).

39 The letter from H. H. the Dalai Lama reads as follows: "This is to certify that Sakyapa Mrs. Dolkar, who once suffered from wild schizophrenic derangement on account of being 'possessed' by certain occult power—was advised by Ladahki Saphod Lhamo to get initiated into exorcism as a [psychotherapeutic] technique. She was then ordained by Taklung Tsetrul Rinpoche and Saphod Lhamo according to formal Tantric rites to be the authentic possessor of Dorje Yüdronma

[a shamanic manifestation of cosmic force] and therefore is a reliable exorcist for [therapeutic] consultation on all mental and physical ills and problems."

40 A detailed report of Mrs. Dolkar's journey from mad woman to healer has been documented in an unpublished manuscript by Fiona Kaul-Connolly titled "Lhamo Dolkar: The Life and Work of the Dorje Yüdronma Oracle," which Mrs. Dolkar gave to me and which led to the investigation of some of the issues discussed in this chapter.

41 *Man* is the center of volition, morality, and emotion and is distinguished from the physical heart (*mutu*), albeit it is located in the area of the heart (Desjarlais 1992, 55–57; Peters 2000, 17, 25).

42 Tibetans most commonly use *me-göd* (wild or untamed man) to describe the yeti (Samuel 1993, 218). They also use *me-chen-po* (great man), *dred-mo* and *che-mo* (types of female bear) (Majupuria and Kumar 1994, 46; Messner 2000, x; Panday 1994, 36), *sogpa* (*sokpa*), a giant demon that looks like an ape, that kills buffalo, and whose eighteen- to twenty-four-inch feet point backward (Macdonald 1976, 323, 338–339 n. 67; Napier 1973, 37), *teh-ima* (man-like thing/bear) (Aharon 1961, 462; Sanderson 1961, 269), or *almas,* a Mongolian term for a large cattle eater (Aharon 1961, 460) as well as a small wildman (Shackley 1983, 98). The Bhutanese frequently use the same term as the Tibetans (*me-göd,* pronounced and often spelled *mi-gyu* in the folktales translated into English), which they say has the appearance of an "ape-man" (Choden 1997, 58). Various Sherpa use *dzu-te* or *juti* (a large, strong, aggressive cattle eater), *ri mi* (mountain man), and *thom* or *chom* (bear), *mi-dre* (man-demon), *mi-bom-po* ([wild] man shaman), and *gang-mi* (glacier man, an expression also used to designate the Himalayan brown bear) (Messner 2000, x; Napier 1973, 58; Nebesky-Wojkowitz 1956, 137; Wangdi 1994, 3, 23, 27). The Lepchas of Sikkim call the yeti *chu-mung* (spirit of the glaciers). To them, the yeti is the Lord of Mountains and Forest Animals and God of the Hunt, and sacrifices are traditionally made to him before the hunt (Lall 1988a, 48). This is only a partial list of the names for the yeti. Some others are referenced in this book and discussed at some length.

43 The term Bönpo, as it is used here, is the name given to the pre-Buddhist indigenous shamanism of Tibet. Sometimes, in the literature, it is called the Bön religion, but it is not a religion; it is shamanism, which does not have a church or an overarching political structure and is highly individualistic (Eliade 1964, 64–65). It is loosely structured, and the only hierarchy that exists is that between guru and disciple shaman. Bön, like other shamanisms, is an oral tradition with a rich folklore and belief system of spirits, demons, and deities. Thus, in the way I am employing Bönpo (or *bombo* in Tamang; sometimes *bompo* among Helambu Sherpa) designates an individual shamanic practitioner. The noun *bön* is directly related to shamanism and is used in the sense of to "pray," "invoke," "present," or "offer" something to deities and spirits (Tucci 1988, 271 n. 2). *Bön* may come from a common source as the term Böd, which is the name for the country of Tibet. The term "Tibetan" is a Western designation for the "people of Böd" (Ekvall 1964, 16; 1968, 1).

44 Sometimes spelled *raksi bompo* or *bompo* in the folklore literature (see Gupta and Nath 1994, 101; also Lall 1988a, 25). My transliteration from Tibetan combines Das (1974, 1116) and Jäschke (1972, 523), which seems closest to the pronunciation of the Tamang residing in the Kathmandu area. It is also commonly translated from classical Tibetan as *rang zin, rang shin,* and *rang shis.* This Tibetan term is sometimes confused with the Sanskrit and Nepali *raksas* or demon.

45 Experiential encounters with the ban jhankri are recorded by anthropologists from many areas in Nepal and with numerous ethnic groups. To cite some of these: from Limbu shamans (Sagant 1976), shamans in the Kalimpong area of India near the Nepali-Indian border (Macdonald 1976), Shorung Sherpa (Paul 1976), Helambu Sherpa (Desjarlais 1992), Magar of the Bhujel Valley in western Nepal (Hitchcock 1976), Sunuwar in central Nepal (Riboli 2000), Thami and Tamang in the Dolakha district (Miller 1997), Tamang residing in Kathmandu (Skafte 1992) and in Boudhanath (Eigner 2001; Peters 1981), and Magar in the Pokhara area (Conton 2001). Ban jhankri abductions and initiatory encounters are nearly pan-Nepali (Desjarlais 1989, 289; Peters 1997a,

48). However, the abduction element of the encounter seems to be more prevalent in eastern and central Nepal and less frequent in western Nepal (Maskarinec 1995, 196–197). As Nepali is the lingua franca of Nepal and is spoken by the great majority of the people, the term ban jhankri is typically used, regardless of the ethnic group's native language. There are, however, local names in many of the native languages. To cite a few examples: in Sunawari, the ban jhankri is called *bashipiumbo* (forest shaman) (Fournier 1976, 119 n. 4); among Helambu Sherpa, *ri-bombo* (mountain shaman) (Desjarlais 1992, 16); to the Limbu *tampungma* (master of forest) and *toksongba* (master of mountain ridges) (Sagant 1976, 69). There are other Nepali names sometimes used for the ban jhankri: *jangali admi* (wildman of the woods), *ban manis* and *ban manche* (forest man, connoting wildness), and *banpa* (forest spirit) (Lall 1988a, 24; Napier 1973, 38). There are also dialectic differences, for example, *ban jhanggari* (Maskarinec 1995, 196, 247).

[46] Ordinary reality (O.R.) and nonordinary reality (N.O.R.) are distinguished by Harner (1990, 46, 50). O.R. is our usual perception of external reality, whereas N.O.R. is accessed through a specific altered state called the "shamanic state of consciousness," which is a spiritual state of conscious perception that is not perceived in the ordinary state of consciousness. The shaman's state of consciousness during a soul journey has many elements in common with "lucid dreams" or "waking dreams" (Krippner, Bogzaran, and de Carvalho 2002, 24; Peters 1982, 34–36; Peters 1989, 130–131; Peters and Price-Williams 1980, 405–406).

[47] For detailed descriptions of these healing methods, see Peters (1995, 57).

[48] Data on Gajendra's experiences was collected during my one-year apprenticeship with him. For a verbatim narrative on one of Gajendra's encounters with the "forest shamans," see Peters (1981, 80–81). In earlier writings, Gajendra was given the pseudonym of Bhirendra to protect his identity. After his death in 1985, I found no need for anonymity, and have since referenced all shamans by their real names for the benefit of persons seeking them out for healing.

49 The ban jhankrini, the wife of the forest shaman, is sometimes known as the *ban bokshini* (forest sorceress) (Riboli 2000, 87) or *lidini* (a cannibalistic fiend) (Lall 1988a, 25). Among Helambu Sherpa and Tamang, she is nyalmo, the same name used for yeti, and is identically described as a semihuman female beast or demon (Lall 1988a, 25; Panday 1994, 36). The *yakshini* (*yaksi*) are of the same class of female deity (Gupta and Nath 1994, 100–101). The ban jhankrini is often called *ban devi* (forest goddess) or ban kali (forest Kali) by Nepalese shamans, just as is the nyalmo yeti. Sometimes she is identified as *dhankini* (spirit sorceress), as distinct from *bokshi* (human sorceress).

50 Thematically similar stories are found across numerous Nepalese tribal and urban settings (Dietrich 1998, 98; Hitchcock 1974, 153–155; 1976, 183–186).

51 The pau are not "possessed" by their spirits, but their psychic veins or channels (tsa) are opened and become infused with their spirits' radiance, powers, and consciousness. Pau Sri-chöd explained that the shaman gets the light but doesn't become the bulb.

52 *The Tibetan Book of the Dead* (or the After-Death Experiences on the Bardo Plane) is an eighth-century text attributed to Padma Sambhava (who is also called Guru Rinpoche), who brought Buddhism to Tibet and is said to have conquered the deities "of the old shamanic faith" (or Bön) and converted them to protectors of Buddhism (dharmapala).

53 Amitabha is the Sanskrit name most often used in Buddhist literature for the Buddha of "boundless light" and eternal life. He is called Nang-wa-tha-ye ("infinite splendor") or Od-pag-me ("infinite light") in Tibetan.

54 Traditionally in Tibet, sand was left at the entrances to the house.

55 Thang Lha (or Nyan Chen Thang Lha) is also regarded as the protective deity of Marpori, the hill upon which the traditional residence of the Dalai Lama, the Potala, is built. Index

INDEX

ABOUT THE AUTHOR

Dr. LARRY PETERS is a world-renowned scholar and initiated shaman in the Tamang-Nepal tradition. He was recipient of the Regent's Fellowship at the University of California, Los Angeles, and an NICCHD post-doctoral fellow at UCLA's Neuropsychiatric Institute. Dr. Peters holds advanced degrees in both anthropology and psychology. He has conducted ethnographic fieldwork in Nepal, China, Mongolia, and Siberia and is a Nepal Research Associate of the Foundation for Shamanic Studies. Dr. Peters has published extensively on shamanism, conducted workshops on Tibetan shamanism in the United States, Europe, and Asia, and for more than sixteen years led experiential initiation journeys to Nepal.